MASTER PLAY
in
CONTRACT
BRIDGE

Terence Reese

Dover Publications, Inc.

New York

IN MEMORY OF MY MOTHER

WHO TAUGHT ME BRIDGE

AND MANY OTHER THINGS

THAT I LEARNED LESS WELL

TERENCE REESE

Published in Canada by General Publishing Company, Ltd., 30 Lesmill Road, Don Mills, Toronto,
Ontario.

This Dover edition, first published in 1974, is an
unabridged and unaltered republication of the work
first published under the title "Master Play" in
1960. The work is republished by special arrangement with the original publisher, George Coffin
Publisher, 257 Trapelo Rd., Waltham, Massachusetts.

International Standard Card Number: 0-486-20336-0
Library of Congress Catalog Card Number: 74-82212

Manufactured in the United States of America
Dover Publications, Inc.
31 East 2nd Street
Mineola, N.Y. 11501

FOREWORD

With several excellent books on card play in print, one may ask, "Why another?" The answer is based on the top-level position occupied by *Master Play* in the literature of bridge.

The most complete and up-to-date textbooks on card play are *Play of the Cards* by Fred Karpin on the elementary level and *Bridge Play from A to Z* by George S. Coffin on the intermediate level. The top level of master strategy was sparsely occupied by specialized works on defense and end games until now. *Master Play* carries on where these other textbooks end.

Terence Reese in his foreword in the British edition says, "I have sought to fill in the picture of what a good player needs to know of technique and, more difficult, to lay a finger on the more subtle effects of style and imagination that make the difference between a player with sound technical knowledge and an expert who is able to improvise and experiment.

"As to sources, my greatest debt is to my friend and colleague, Alfred P. Sheinwold of New York, a writer of exceptional clarity and perception with whom I have exchanged ideas so freely over the years that neither of us could say which began where.

"In reading proofs I have had the benefit of a most careful survey by Mr. Albert Dormer. In that connection may I, from experience of previous books and articles, make the following observation to a certain type of critic: when half way through a hand a defensive play of some sort is recommended, it is not a refutation ('your problem is wrong because . . .') to point out that if the declarer had stood on his head and kicked his heels in the air, he could still have made the contract by some other means. One aims to present a lesson in practical play, not an exercise in double dummy."

DECEPTION gets top billing with 21 deals. This suggests that a winning player needs a stiff upper lip and a larcenous heart. Victory in many deals cannot be obtained by brute force alone.

I recall an incident in 1930 in the late Scott K. Wainwright's Copley Square bridge studio in Boston, Mass. The late John F. Barry, attorney and famous chess player who once beat world chess champion Paul Morphy in an exhibition match, was my RHO in 4 ♠. Barry was equally good at bridge, albeit conservative. Holding ♠ A-Q-3, I laid down the ace to look at dummy. What I saw there was a shock, ♠ K-J-5 over my poor queen instead of with declarer as advertised by his auction. So quickly I banged down the ♠ 3 next with all the appearance of utter disinterest in trumps, and Barry stalled in the longest trance in bridge history. Finally he took the wrong view and flew with the king and my partner discarded. Later Barry lost two more tricks for one down. Had I shifted to another suit at Trick Two or had I not opened the ♠ A, instead leaving Barry to his own devices, surely he would have decided to finesse through my queen.

Next of import are 18 RUFF deals and 16 HOLD deals on the technical background of strategy and tactics. The fourth and last copiously illustrated type is ELIMINATIONS (X) with 13 examples offered perhaps not so much for their value in practice as for their artistry.

GEORGE S. COFFIN

CONTENTS

PART I

PART II

AROUND THE TRUMP SUIT

PART III

THE FIELD OF TACTICS

PART IV

MATTERS OF TECHNIQUE

APPENDIX

INDEX TO PLAY TYPES

ARRANGED BY GEORGE S. COFFIN

Each deal in this book is marked with a play type file letter, as A for Avoidance, B for Blocking, etc. The deal numbers are given in the Coffin Index below for purposes of comparison with *Bridge Play from A to Z*, the modern bridge dictionary.

A second purpose of Coffin indexing is to reveal which types of plays Terence Reese considers the most important in top-level play as indicated by the number of his illustrations of each play type.

INDEX TO BRIDGE RHYMES AND CARTOONS

BY GEORGE S. COFFIN AND OTHERS

PART I

INFERENCE AND HYPOTHESIS

Chapter 1

"HOW COULD I TELL?"

"There was no way in which I could tell." How often is it true? Early in the play, not often; towards the end, never. Players who throw the wrong card after ten or eleven tricks, then make this excuse, are simply confessing that they have missed some inference or been misled by their partners, for there must always be an indication of some sort.

These first two chapters are concerned, not with any form of technical play, but with the process of reasoning that will lead a player to the right choice when he seems to be faced with a dilemma. Mostly, this is a defensive problem. A defender who has to make a critical play should tentatively select what seems the best line and then examine it in the light of the following test:—

1. Is there anything in my partner's play up to now that does not fit in with the picture of the hand on which my intended play is based?

2. Is there anything in the declarer's play that does not fit in with my general picture?

3. Have I counted the declarer's possible tricks and am I satisfied that the play I have in mind, in so far as it contains any risk, must be made now?

There are few problems that cannot be resolved by a player who will direct his mind to each of the three questions above. In the first example West finds the answer by applying test no. 1. The full hand is shown, but the conscientious reader will study the situation as it appears to West when he has the lead at the fourth trick.

South played in 4 ♠, having supported North's hearts on the way. West opened ♣ 5 and the ace won. East played ◇ K, then ◇ 7, on which South false-carded the 6, then 8. West won and had to decide whether to try to cash a third diamond or the ♣ K.

Deal 1

North, dummy
♠ Q 6
♡ A Q J 9 5
◇ J 9 4
♣ Q 7 4

O - 4 ♠

West
♠ 10 5
♡ 8 6 2
◇ A 5 2
♣ K 10 6 5 3

East
♠ J 9 4
♡ 7 3
◇ K Q 10 7
♣ A 9 8 2

South, declarer
♠ A K 8 7 3 2
♡ K 10 4
◇ 8 6 3
♣ J

"South might well have dropped the jack of clubs from J-x," West thought to himself. "I couldn't bear it if he were to ruff a third diamond and discard a club on dummy's hearts. It's a guess, no one can blame me if I do the wrong thing."

So West tried to cash ♣ K and the contract was made. With all the evidence before you, can you say how West should have known which suit to play?

No sure inference could be drawn from the bidding or from declarer's play: South's shape could have been 6-3-2-2. But what of East? Suppose that he had held ◇ K-Q-10-x-x: would his defence have been the same?

In that case East would have known that the defence could take only two diamond tricks. It would have been his clear duty, after making ◇ K, to cash ◇ Q, intending to hold the lead and switch to clubs.

Once a player directs his mind to the problem, this is not a difficult inference to draw. Players make mistakes because they do not begin to think along the right lines.

A universal example occurs when the right-hand defender, East, fails to lead up to obvious weakness in the dummy. The immediate inference should be that he has a high card of the suit, ace or king, and can stand a lead from his partner.

The next hand is more difficult. The clue is unsubstantial and is valid only with a first-class partner.

Deal 2 ✕

	♠ Q 6 5 3	O - 4 ♡
	♡ K 8 4 2	
	◇ A	
	♣ K J 10 4	

♠ 7 4   ♠ A K J 10 2
♡ Q J   ♡ 9
◇ 8 6 3 2   ◇ J 10 9 5
♣ A 9 8 5 2   ♣ 7 6 3

♠ 9 8
♡ A 10 7 6 5 3
◇ K Q 7 4
♣ Q

At most tables in a pairs contest South played in 4 ♡ after North had opened the bidding with 1 ♣ and East had made an overcall of 1 ♠. The defence usually began with a spade to the 10, then ♠ K followed by ♠ A. South ruffed high, crossed to ♡ K, and discarded his club on ♠ Q, so making the contract. It would be no better for East to lead a low spade at trick 3, for then South would discard his losing club.

At one table an expert East realised that it might be necessary to cash a club before leading a third spade. He won the first trick with ♠ 10 and played well by returning a club to his partner's ace. Had West now returned a spade, a third spade would have established a certain trump trick for the defence.

West had other ideas, however. After winning with ♣ A he returned a club for his partner to ruff. This gave declarer an overtrick.

West's explanation sounded quite plausible. "When you won with the ten of spades and switched to a club, naturally I thought you had a singleton. It seemed so obvious for you to continue spades."

Can you see any weakness in his argument? It is a good test.

The answer is that if East had had a singleton club, and so wanted a club return, his right play at the first trick would have been to win with ♠ A, not the 10. The play of the ace would have suggested that there was no future in spades.

A Hint from Declarer

In the next example a misguided false card by declarer is the clue to the defence.

South was in three notrump and West opened ♡ 3. Some players do not like to lead a low card from four rags, but it is a debatable point, and to lead fourth best is certainly not wrong.

Deal 3

	♠ J 10	O - 3 NT
	♡ J 2	
	◇ K Q 8 7	
	♣ A Q 9 8 4	

♠ K 4 3		♠ 8 7 2
♡ 8 6 4 3		♡ A K 7
◇ J 4		◇ A 10 9 5 3
♣ J 7 6 2		♣ 10 3

	♠ A Q 9 6 5
	♡ Q 10 9 5
	◇ 6 2
	♣ K 5

Declarer played the 2 from dummy, East played the king, and now South dropped the 9.

South's idea, if at all clearly formed, was to make the opponents think that he was short in hearts and to encourage a heart continuation. To an observant opponent, however, quite a different impression was conveyed. East could tell from the lead of the 3, with the 2 in dummy, that West had only four hearts. Therefore South's play of the 9 must be a false card and the inference was that he was well upholstered in that suit.

On this reasoning East switched to a low diamond, playing his partner for the ◇ J. This play won five tricks for the defence, for when West came in with ♠ K he was able to return a diamond to his partner's ◇ A-10.

Forcing an Early Decision

Declarers are not always so heavy-minded. This is a hand from Britain vs. Austria in the European Championship of 1950:—shown below.

Deal 4

	♠ 5	Q - 4 ♠
	♡ Q 8 6	
	◇ A Q 10 4	
	♣ K 9 7 5 2	

♠ 10 8 6 4 3		♠ 7
♡ A 9 5		♡ K J 4 3
◇ K 9 6 3		◇ J 8 7 2
♣ 4		♣ J 8 6 3

	♠ A K Q J 9 2
	♡ 10 7 2
	◇ 5
	♣ A Q 10

South dealt at game all. The British North-South played in 4 ♠ and after a club lead made the contract by finessing ◇ Q for a heart discard.

At the other table the Austrian South, Karl Schneider, opened 4 ♠. West doubled and led ◇ 3. Declarer should perhaps have risked the finesse, but in practice he won with the ace, led ♠ 5 and played ♠ 9, putting West on play before he had had a chance to observe his partner's discards. West laid down ♡ A, but the message from his partner's 4 was not altogether clear. After some thought West switched to a club, hoping that partner had the ace.

East played low, South won with the 10, drew trumps, and won ♣ A, producing this position:—

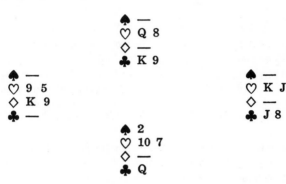

On the last trump a heart was thrown from dummy and East also had to let go a heart. Then South cashed ♣ Q, exited with a heart, and won the last trick with dummy's ♣ K.

To what extent was West to blame? His play would have been right had South held the ♡ K and something like ♣ Q-10-x. With that sort of holding, would South have ducked the first round of trumps? He would have had no reason to. The object of that play was clearly to lose the trump trick at a moment when West might find the wrong switch. From West's point of view, South must be hoping to discard hearts on clubs, not clubs on hearts.

Declarer played this hand with great skill: not so much the end game, which developed automatically, as the gambit at trick 2. He felt sure, of course, that West's double included a trump trick, the more so as the opening lead suggested that West did not hold ♡ A-K.

It is often a good move for the declarer to give up a critical trick early. Deal 5 is another example:—

Deal 5

	♠ Q 9 5	O - 6 ♠
	♡ Q 4	
	◇ A K J 10 3	
	♣ Q 10 6	

♠ 8 7		♠ 6 3 2
♡ 10 7 5 3 2		♡ J 8
◇ 5 2		◇ Q 9 4
♣ A J 8 4		♣ K 7 5 3 2

	♠ A K J 10 4
	♡ A K 9 6
	◇ 8 7 6
	♣ 9

At game all North dealt and bid 1 ◇. South forced with 2 ♠ and North raised to 3 ♠. Without further communication to the enemy South bid 6 ♠.

With no attractive lead, West opened ♠ 8. South won with the jack and at once finessed the diamond. This was good play, for the finesse had to be faced sooner or later and the sooner it was taken the better the chance that East, if he did not hold ♣ A, would make the wrong return. If three rounds of trumps are drawn, for example, West has a chance to discard a low heart.

When he won with ◇ Q East realised that he had to find his partner's ace. With what seemed to him an open choice he led a heart. "There was nothing to guide me," he said afterwards.

Nothing, except that on no reasonable construction of the cards could South be missing ♡ A and have so few hearts that they could be discarded on the diamonds. That would give West a six- or seven-card suit headed by the ace, which undoubtedly he would have led. A singleton club, on the other hand, South might well have.

To Bed with an Ace

When the defenders have two top tricks to make against a slam contract, they often have a problem in finding them soon enough. Every player has had the experience of sitting with an ace after his partner has won an early trick, waiting in agony for partner to make the right lead. This is especially true when the defenders have two aces—something they do not expect.

Even though this particular trap is avoided (in favour of many others) by addicts of the Blackwood convention, it is sometimes difficult to stay out of a slam when all the high cards are held except for two aces.

Deal 6

     ♠ K 8 7 3   O - 6 NT
     ♡ Q
     ◇ K Q J 8 4
     ♣ K Q 6

♠ 6 4 2   ♠ A 10 5
♡ 8 6 3 2   ♡ 7 5 4
◇ A 10 7 6   ◇ 9 2
♣ 7 4   ♣ 10 9 8 5 2

     ♠ Q J 9
     ♡ A K J 10 9
     ◇ 5 3
     ♣ A J 3

On this occasion South opened 1 ♡, North bid 2 ◇ and South 2 NT. With 16 points and a five-card suit North made a slam try of 4 NT. As South had a fair hand for his bidding up to date he took a chance on 6 NT, and there they were with abundant tricks but two aces missing.

West opened ♣ 7. South won with jack and led a low diamond on which West naturally played low. Dummy's jack held the trick and a low spade was returned to the queen. Declarer then led ♠ J and East won with ace. Now East led a heart and South was able to run off twelve tricks by way of three spades, five hearts, one diamond and three clubs.

East explained that he placed South with ◇ A-x-x and thought the only chance was to win a heart trick quickly. Can you say where that argument breaks down?

Suppose that East had been right in his analysis of the diamond situation. That would give the declarer five tricks in diamonds, three in spades and (in all probability) three in clubs. He still could not make the slam without the ♡ A. So, there could be no advantage in leading a heart now: if East had arrived at that conclusion, he might have thought again about the ◇ A.

Counting the Tricks

On the last hand the defender's play was based not so much on inference as on counting declarer's possible tricks. These are some more hands on which the obvious play will fail and the defender will do the right thing only if he keeps an intelligent count and looks deeply into the position.

Deal 7

♠ J 10 8 2
♡ 9 7 2
◇ A 5
♣ A Q 10 4

N - 4 ♠

♠ 6 5
♡ J 8 5
◇ J 9 7 4
♣ 7 6 3 2

♠ 9 3
♡ A K 10 6 4
◇ K 10 2
♣ K J 5

♠ A K Q 7 4
♡ Q 3
◇ Q 8 6 3
♣ 9 8

South played in 4 ♠ after East had opened 1 ♡. The hearts were led and continued, and South ruffed the third round. After drawing trumps South led ♣ 8, running it to East's jack.

An average player in East's position, noting that a heart or club return would certainly give up a trick, would try a diamond.

As East, in actual play, was not hopeful of finding his partner with the ◇ Q, he studied the other possibilities. In most elimination positions, when a defender has to choose between conceding a ruff and discard and leading into a tenace, it is better to allow the ruff and discard. Thinking along these lines, East constructed for South a 5-2-3-3 hand, including ◇ Q. If that were South's hand, a heart would not help him: if he discarded a club from his own hand he would have to lose a diamond, and if he discarded a diamond from dummy he would have to lose a club.

Having reached this point in his analysis, East led a heart, but that was not good enough against the actual distribution. South ruffed in his own hand, discarding a diamond from table. Then he led a club to the ace and established another club trick by leading through East's king. Two diamonds were ruffed and one went away on the established ♣ 10.

The play that looked the least attractive of the three would have worked against any distribution. South was known to have six cards in the minor suits. If a club return gave him two discards, he would still have to lose a diamond. The short way to this conclusion was to reflect that South had on top five tricks in spades, one in diamonds and, at most, three in clubs; that is only nine, so he would have to lose a diamond after a club return.

On the next hand South made the play more difficult by a well-judged false card.

Deal 8   ♠ J 5   C - 6 ♡
                          ♡ K J 8 7
                          ◇ 9 4 2
                          ♣ A K 10 6

♠ K Q 9 8   ♠ 7 4 3 2
♡ 5 4   ♡ 2
◇ K 10 6 3   ◇ J 8 7 5
♣ 9 4 2   ♣ Q J 8 3

                          ♠ A 10 6
                          ♡ A Q 10 9 6 3
                          ◇ A Q
                          ♣ 7 5

South was in 6 ♡ and West opened ♠ K. South won, drew trumps, and ruffed out the clubs. When this suit had been eliminated he exited with ♠ 10. That was quite a clever play, for it created the impression that he had no more spades; otherwise the play of the spade 10 would be giving up a certain (though in fact valueless) trick.

When West took the second spade he stopped to count declarer's shape. He placed him with two spades, six hearts, three diamonds and two clubs. If that were right the defence would have to make a diamond trick, and West saw no reason not to play for an extra trick should his partner hold ◇ Q. Accordingly, he led a low diamond, and South was home.

All one can say of this hand is that West was taken in by the false card. Once he had started to count, he should have realised that a spade continuation could not possibly present South with the contract.

The British Ladies won their section of the European Championship in 1951, but one of them fell down on a very instructive point of defence when the following hand was played :—

FIDA

By Elsie Dickson, Pendleton, Oregon
ACBL Bulletin, May 1955

Oh, deliver me please from partners like Ida,
Constantly stuttering, muttering "fida!"
"Fida led trumps, we'da made game . . ."
"Fida done that . . . oh, dear, what a shame!"

And, also the players who talk about "fyouda . . ."
They make me as hot as the sun in Bermuda . . .
"Fyouda finessed, youda brought home that slam . . ."
"Really now Partner, you played like a ham!"

Deal 9

♠ 10 5
♡ 7 3
◇ A Q J 10
♣ A K Q 10 4

O - 3 NT

♠ A J 9 7
♡ A J 2
◇ 6 4 3 2
♣ J 7

♠ K 4 2
♡ K 9 6 5
◇ 9 7
♣ 8 6 3 2

♠ Q 8 6 3
♡ Q 10 8 4
◇ K 8 5
♣ 9 5

North was the dealer, and the bidding went as follows:—

South	North
—	1 ♣
1 ♡	2 ◇
2 NT	3 NT

West led ♠ 7, East won with king and returned the 4. Had East held four spades she would have returned the fourth best, so West could tell from the fall of the cards that South still held ♠ Q-8. West accordingly switched to a diamond, hoping to find her partner with the king; thereupon South ran off nine tricks.

Most players would have done the same as West, but deeper consideration would have shown that the hearts should be tried first. The point is that if South does not hold ◇ K she cannot steal the game. Assume, at worst, that South has a heart suit headed by K-Q-10; she may win the 10 and return a heart, but now West will play a diamond and South will be unable to regain the lead unless she holds ◇ K. (It is true that from West's point of view, South may have an entry with ♣ 9, but in that case dummy will be bereft of entries after the ◇ A and top clubs have been played.) In short, the diamonds can wait.

PRAYER	CONFESSION
Let the experts make slam cues, Lay traps wiley in the thickets;	I am a rabbit who has the habit Of playing bridge for money.
Signals, endplays, squeezes use: But let ME hold all the tickets!	I say I get by, but I know I lie, So please don't tell my Honey!

Chapter 2

DISCOVERY, ASSUMPTION, AND CONCEALMENT

The previous chapter covered ways in which a player could draw inferences from the evidence before him; this chapter, with ways of discovering, concealing, and in some cases imagining, the evidence.

Most players would find the following hand straight-forward:—

Deal 10

♠ 10 8 4 2
♡ K 9 8 3
◇ A Q 4 3
♣ Q

C - 6 ♠

♣ 9 led

♠ A Q J 9 7 5
♡ —
◇ 6 5 2
♣ A K 7 4

At love all South opens 1 ♠ fourth hand. North, having passed, raises to 4 ♠, and South, taking a fair gamble, goes straight to 6 ♠. Prospects of reaching Seven with any certainty are remote, and there is no point in giving information to the opponents.

West leads ♣ 9, won by queen on table. South will look first to see if there is anything to be said for cashing ♠ A and playing for some elimination position. The chances of this are remote, so he may judge that the hand depends on one of two finesses and lead a spade to finesse queen.

It is possible to improve on that play. At trick 2 declarer should lead ♡ K from dummy. Say that East covers with ace; South ruffs and finesses ◇ Q. East wins with the king and leads ♠ 6. Now South has discovered for sure that East holds ♡ A and ◇ K. Since West opened ♣ 9 it is probable also that East holds the ♣ J-10; if South wants to look still further, he can place East with intermediate cards in both hearts and diamonds, for had West held a solid sequence in either suit he would presumably have led it.

In short, South has built up for East a hand on which, if it contained the ♠ K as well, he might well have opened the bidding third hand. Having reached this point, South may decline the spade finesse and play to drop king singleton.

This was a somewhat artificial example of this type of play, but the principle of discovery is extremely common in all play. It will arise in many later examples.

Making a Necessary Assumption

Not many players realise that there are different kinds of assumption. Here is an example of a situation in which declarer holds a side suit of J-x-x in dummy, A-Q-x-x-x in his own hand. Since he can not afford to lose a trick in the suit, declarer has to assume that the player sitting over the J-x-x holds K-x. His estimate of the distribution and his play of the trump suit are based on that purely hypothetical premise.

That is an interesting and important theme that deserves more than one example. There are some more hands of the same type below.

Deal 11   ♠ A 9 5 2   F - 3 ♠ or 4 ♠
                           ♡ J 7 4
                    K   ◊ Q J 8 3   *assume*
                           ♣ 6 2   D-K in E or W
    ♡ K led   C-A   "   "
                           ♠ K Q 10 6 4
                           ♡ 8 3
                           ◊ A 4
                    A   ♣ K J 7 5

South opens 1 ♠ fourth hand, and we will assume, first, that he finishes in 3 ♠. West opens ♡ K and follows with a low heart to his partner's ace. To the third trick East leads a low club.

From the play so far, there is no guide to the position of the club honors. The play is a guess in a sense, yet there is a subtle reason why South should go up with the king.

So long as he does not lose two tricks in clubs, South can afford to lose the diamond finesse. He should build up a picture of the hand on the assumption that it is wrong. West is already marked with ♡ K-Q; give him the ◊ K as well, and it becomes unlikely that he will have the ♣ A. That is why, in 3 ♠, the king is the right play.   (E)

Now let us assume that South is in 4 ♠.

The defence goes the same way as before. West leads ♡ K and follows with a heart to his partner's ace. East leads a low club.

Now the situation is reversed. With two tricks lost in hearts and at least one certain loser in clubs, South must assume that ◊ K is right. That marks East with ♡ A and (hypothetically) the ◊ K. Give him the ♣ A as well, and he will have likely material for an opening hand. Accordingly, South should be disposed to place the ♣ A on the other side and should finesse the jack.   (in W)

For most readers this will be an entirely new line of thought, so it may be well to re-state the underlying principle:—

When a contract depends on the positions of two or three key cards it

*often helps to make a definite assumption about one of them. If you can
afford to have it wrong, assume that it is wrong; if you must have it
right, assume that it is right and build up your picture of the opposing
hands on that basis.*

This is another and perhaps more difficult example of "second degree"
assumption:—

♠ A K 10 6 3
♡ Q 5
◇ Q 4
♣ K Q 6 2

♡ K led

♠ Q J 9 4 2
♡ 7
◇ A J 6 3
♣ 8 7 4

West deals at game all and the bidding goes:

South	*West*	*North*	*East*
—	1 ♡	Double	2 ♡
3 ♠	Pass	4 ♠	All pass

West leads ♡ K and continues with ♡ A. South ruffs and draws trumps
in two rounds. What should he play next? The contract will fail only if
South loses two tricks in clubs and one in diamonds. Suppose that he leads
a club, which looks obvious. If East holds the ♣ A, then surely West will
hold the ◇ K and South will be defeated. Playing a diamond first, on the
other hand, he is completely safe. If West holds ◇ K and puts it up, there
will be two club discards on declarer's ◇ A-J. But if East holds ◇ K,
then assuredly West will hold the ♣ A.

It is a puzzling but instructive hand. This is the distribution against
which South has to guard:—

Deal 12 ✳

♠ A K 10 6 3
♡ Q 5
◇ Q 4
♣ K Q 6 2

F - 4 ♠

♠ 5
♡ A K J 8 4 3
◇ K 8 5
♣ J 9 5

♠ 8 7
♡ 10 9 6 2
◇ 10 9 7 2
♣ A 10 3

♠ Q J 9 4 2
♡ 7
◇ A J 6 3
♣ 8 7 4

*assume
D-K in West
play diamond
before club*

After the last two examples the next hand will seem quite easy:—

Deal 13

♠ 8 5 3 2
♡ K 7 4
◇ A 10 6
♣ 8 5 4

F - 5 ◇

♠ K led

S - Q

C - A ?

♠ A
♡ A Q J 2
◇ Q J 9 7 5 4
♣ K 6

D - K

C - A

South plays in 5 ◇ against passing opponents. West opens ♠ K and South wins the ace. If South finesses a diamond and loses, and a club comes through, he may find himself losing two clubs and a diamond. It is unlikely, however, that West, in addition to ♠ K-Q and ♣ A, will have the ◇ K guarded. South should therefore reject the diamond finesse and go up with the ace; if he returns a diamond and the trick is won by West, he can be quite sure that the ♣ A will be right for him.

If he drops the singleton ◇ K from East, he may have some difficulty in explaining his play—but that is another matter!

Upside-down Inferences

There is an intersting group of positions, seldom written about, that give rise to what may be thought of as indirect, backward, or "upside-down" inferences: that is to say, inferences based on an opponent's failure to make an accepted play. This is a standard example:—

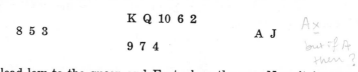

8 5 3 　　　K Q 10 6 2 　　　A J

9 7 4

You lead low to the queen and East plays the ace. Now it is normally correct play for East, if he holds A-x, to play low, so that declarer will have a guess on the next round. Therefore, when East wins with ace, there are grounds for assuming that he has ace alone or A-J. Of course, if declarers were constantly to draw that inference, it would become good play for a defender to play the ace from A-x; it is a world of bluff and double bluff.

This is a similar position:—

Q J 9 5 3

8 6 4   K 10

A 7 2

The queen is led from dummy and East plays the king. Now with K-x it is usual to play low, so that declarer will have to guess whether to follow with the jack or with a low card. So, when the king goes up, it is fair to assume that East has K-10 doubleton or king alone.

There are many inferences to be drawn from this familiar holding:—

A J 9 3

Q 10 4   K 8 2

7 6 5

South leads the 7 and, if West plays low, the best mathematical play for declarer is to insert the 9. This gains against K-10 or Q-10 in West, loses only to K-Q.

It is standard play, however, for West to go up second hand with the queen (or with the king from K-10-x). This may create entry difficulties for the declarer and it also gives him a guess when on the next round he leads low and West plays the 4. In general, declarer should stick to his original intention and finesse the 9.

Now suppose that the cards are like this:—

A J 9 3

K Q 4   10 8 2

7 6 5

On the lead of the 7 West will generally play low, expecting declarer to finesse the 9. But should he? Here we have a typical upside-down inference: West's play of the 4, for most players, practically denies a holding of Q-10-x or K-10-x. On that reasoning there are good grounds to put up the jack.

Here again there is no end to the bluff and double bluff that would arise if all players were equally skillful. However, the situation remains, fortunate for learned readers, unfortunate for impecunious authors, that a large proportion of the bridge-playing public does not study the latest developments. The intelligent reader can keep a jump ahead of those players.

K 10 9

Q J   8 6 4 3

A 7 5 2

This is a side suit at a trump contract and East, after elimination play, has to open up the suit. He leads low, perforce, and the queen loses to the king. Here we have an example of a defender having failed to make an expected play. From J-x-x-x or Q-x-x-x a good player in East's position would lead the honor. There are therefore grounds for placing West with Q-J and for declining the finesse on the way back. This inference, of course, would not exist if East were less than a good player.

There are a number of quiet inferences that are not infallible but are well worth noting.

A Q J 4
7 6 2

South leads low and finesses the queen. East wins with the king. Does that mean anything? Unless there are tactical reasons that would force East to take the king in any event, he will, if a good player, generally hold off the finesse on the first round. The exception to this occurs when he has K-x. There is therefore a reasonably sound inference that the suit will divide 4—2.

A Q 6 3
K 5

Quite early in the play at notrump a defender makes a discard in the suit shown. Do you think to yourself "Perhaps he has discarded from four and they are all good now"? Almost always the player who has made the discard has five of the suit; if he discards twice, then he has six. Such inferences can be of great value in counting the hand at an early stage. This is a more spectacular example:—

K Q 9 6 3
8 5 4

South plays in 6 NT and West, who has to make an early discard, throws the 2 of the suit of which the K-Q-9-6-3 are showing on the table. What does that mean? Almost certainly that West has all five outstanding cards; with no other holding would he throw a card of the suit so early.

Concealing the Evidence

Just as the declarer must try to learn the secrets of the defence, so must the defenders try to keep their secrets. There is no department of the game in which the difference between an average good player and a top-class expert is more clearly marked.

A first-class player, from his experience, will generally recognise quite soon what is going to be the critical point of a hand. He will think of ways to make declarer go wrong. His strategy may begin with the opening lead, as on the following hand:—

Deal 14

                        ♠ K J 4 3   F - 5 ♣
                        ♡ 10 5
                        ◇ 10 8 6
                        ♣ K J 10 4

    ♠ 9 7 5 2   ♠ Q 8 6
    ♡ Q 8 3   ♡ A 7 4
    ◇ A K Q 4   ◇ J 9 7 3 2
    ♣ 7 5   ♣ 9 2

                        ♠ A 10
                        ♡ K J 9 6 2
                        ◇ 5
                        ♣ A Q 8 6 3

South	North
1 ♡	1 ♠
2 ♣	3 ♣
3 ♠	4 ♣
5 ♣	

Now if West opens the ◇ K and follows with the ace (or ace followed by king if that is his convention), declarer will scarcely go wrong in the critical point of the hand, which is the heart finesse. If West opens the ◇ K and follows low, that will be slightly better. Best of all is for West to open the ◇ Q and follow with the low one. West can be sure from the bidding that declarer has, at most, a singleton diamond. There is no reason for West to play his diamonds in the conventional order; his plan from the first should be to conceal his strength in that suit.

When West opens with ◇ Q and follows with the low one it is at least possible that declarer (whatever he makes of East's play of the 9 at trick 2) will place the high diamonds with East; if he does, then he will take the wrong view in hearts.

Many strategic moves by the defence revolve around the queen of trumps.

Deal 15

♠ A 10 5 2
♡ 8 3 2
◇ Q 6 4
♣ K 9 7

F - 4 ♠

♠ Q 9 7
♡ 10 9 6
◇ J 9
♣ J 8 6 4 2

♠ 6
♡ A K Q 5
◇ 10 7 5 3 2
♣ Q 10 5

♠ K J 8 4 3
♡ J 7 4
◇ A K 8
♣ A 3

South	West	North	East
—	—	Pass	Pass
1 ♠	Pass	2 ♠	Pass
3 ◇	Pass	4 ♠	(final bid)

West opens ♡ 10. If East takes the three hearts and plays a diamond, South will note at once that East has turned up with nine points. If his discovery technique is good, South will play three rounds of clubs before tackling spades and will find that East has ♣ Q as well. That will seem to mark West with the ♠ Q and declarer will finesse correctly.

East's best play after the heart is to take the ace and queen, then switch to a diamond. This play will leave open the possibility (from South's point of view) that West started with ♡ K-10-9-x-x; it will also suggest that East is short in hearts. Certainly South will have no reason to take the trump finesse against West.

The next hand was played at notrump and East-West had to play a brainy game to defeat the contract.

FIXED

The waiter grunted at a hand,
North-South and East-West stand
Scrawled upon the table cloth
In messy ink. Should make him wroth.

He did not know the loss of tricks
By the players in all their fix.
For by his view the great misplay
Was they'd left no tip his way.

PSYCHIC BIDS

Have you a partner? Bedam I have
And we were poorly mated.
One night I psyched and psiked and syked
And siked; and now we're separated.

One monthly game for master points
I met him on Round Three.
"Good Evening, Sir!" said I to him.
"Drop dead, you jerk," snapped he.

Deal 16

♠ 9 3
♡ A Q
♢ A Q 10 7 6 4
♣ 9 8 6

V - 3 NT

♠ 10 4 2
♡ J 10 8 5 3 2
♢ J 3
♣ A 5

♠ A K 8 6 5
♡ 7 4
♢ 9 5
♣ K J 7 4

♠ Q J 7
♡ K 9 6
♢ K 8 2
♣ Q 10 3 2

North dealt at love all and the bidding went:—

South	West	North	East
—	—	1 ♢	1 ♠
1 NT	2 ♡	3 ♢	Pass
3 NT	Pass	Pass	Pass

West led ♠ 2 (correct from 10-x-x in partner's suit) and East had to decide at once whether to play for setting tricks in spades or clubs. One possibility was to win with ace or king and return a low spade, hoping that South started with Q-10-x and would finesse the 10. It seemed more likely, however, that South, who had bid notrump twice, would have a secure guard in spades. Moreover, if he had Q-10-x, he would probably take the right view.

East therefore won with ♠ K and played ♣ K followed by ♣ 4. He was trying to create the impression that West had led from ♠ A-x-x and that East himself held ♠ K-x-x-x-x and ♣ A-K-x-x. South fell into the trap and went up with ♣ Q; thus the defenders took two spade and three club tricks.

A more experienced player in South's position would have avoided this mistake. The deceptive play in clubs is well known in expert circles.

Apart from that, there was a reasonable inference that East's clubs were not A-K-x-x. With that holding his natural play, if he was going to attack clubs, would have been a low one. Good players think of those things. That is why good players acquire the reputation of being good guessers.

Chapter 3

THE PRINCIPLE OF RESTRICTED CHOICE

Early in the nineteen-fifties Alan Truscott drew attention in a magazine article to a principle of play whose effect had been dimly perceived but which in general has not been carried through to its conclusion.

Compare these two situations:—

(1) A 10 7 3   (2) A 9 7 3
      K Q 5   K Q 5

In the first example declarer plays off the K-Q and follows with the 5. Both opponents have followed with low cards and now South has to decide whether to finesse the 10 or play for the drop. The odds slightly favor playing for the drop of the jack. The only clue is that the player on the right has one more unknown card than the player on the left. (It is true that a 4—2 split is *a priori* more probable than 3—3, but among the 4—2 splits are those in which the jack is held doubleton, and those possibilities are now excluded.)

In (2) declarer plays off the K-Q, dropping 10-x from his right. He follows with the 5 and when West plays low he has a similar choice, whether to finesse or play for the jack to drop. Are the odds in relation to this finesse much the same as in example (1)?

It would surprise most players to be told that the finesse, instead of being odds against, was now about 2:1 on. While there are different ways of expressing why this should be so, the simplest is to say that if East had held J-10-x then half the time he would have played the jack on the first round. The fact that he has played the 10 affords a fifty per cent presumption that he began with 10-x and not with J-10-x.

The same sort of reasoning can be applied to many situations with which players are much more familiar. For example:—

A Q J 9 7 3   *finesse*   10
   10 8 4 2

South leads the 10 and West follows with the 5. Now two cards are missing, the 6 and the king, and one might say: "East can have the singleton king just as well as the singleton 6, so I will go up with the ace."

Most players know that to play for the drop is well against the odds, even if one leaves out of consideration the possibility of a 3—0 division. It is not accurate to say that East is as likely to have the singleton king as the singleton 6. If West had held the 6—5 originally he could equally have played the 6 on the first round. If he had held the K-5, then his choice would have been restricted: he would have been bound to play the 5.

This is another very common situation where almost all players know the right play by instinct or from precept:—

A J 10 7 5
9 8 4 2

South leads the 9 and loses to the king or queen in East. On the next round he should, of course, finessse again. Since East could have played either card indifferently from K-Q, the fact that he has played one affords an indication that he does not hold the other.

Here is one more situation where players are guided, consciously or not, by the principle of restricted choice:—

K 10 9 5 3
7 2

After a finesse of the 9 has lost to the jack or queen, one finesses the 10 on the next round. Since two honors are outstanding, the ace and the queen-or-jack, why not go up with the king? The answer is the same: East's play of one of the middle honors affords a presumption that he does not hold the other.

The a priori *Expectations*

Arguments of this sort can be confusing and it may help to reflect in connection with all these examples that the recommended play coincides with the *a priori* expectation. In the last example, the chance that East should hold A-J-x or A-Q-x exceeds the chance of his having begun with Q-J-x. In the same way, going back to examine (2) above, the likelihood of East's holding J-x or 10-x clearly exceeds the likelihood of his holding precisely J-10-x.

Some Unexpected Conclusions

Understanding of the principle under discussion will resolve many problems that cause indecision at the table.

A 10 8 6 4 2
K 9 5

The king play drops queen from East. Now, should South play East for Q-J doubleton or for Queen alone? The finesse is almost twice as likely to succeed as the play for the drop. Once again (indeed, it must always be so if the reasoning is correct) the *a priori* expectation of finding East with singleton queen or jack is higher than of finding him with Q-J.

The probabilities are not so easy to assess when South has one card fewer in his two hands:—

A 10 8 6 4
K 9 5

Once again East drops an honor under the king on the first round. Now, while East's play of the jack (or queen) affords a presumption that he does not hold the other honor, declarer must take into consideration the fact that a 3—2 split of the five outstanding cards is appreciably more probable than 4—1. Nevertheless, the finesse is still appreciably the better chance. Q-J dry is only one out of ten possible doubleton combinations. Singleton queen and singleton jack combined represent two out of five possible singletons. Thus, although a doubleton in East's hand is more likely than a singleton, the precise doubleton Q-J is still at the end of the queue.

Note the difference that can arise from these two situations:—

    (1) A Q 8 6 4   (2) A Q 9 6 4
        J 7 5 3   J 7 5 3

In (1) South leads the jack, which is headed by the king and ace, East drops the 9 or 10. In accordance with the principle under review, the odds favor a finesse of the 8 on the next round, and East's play of the 9 affords a presumption that he did not begin with 10-9.

In (2) the jack is followed by king and ace, and East drops the 8. Now it is an open question whether declarer should finesse or play to drop the 10. East's play of the 8 tells nothing about the 10. If he began with 10-8, his choice on the first round was restricted; with 10-9 it was open.

The next example is instructive:—

        Q 9 7 6 4 2
        A 5

South's ace lead drops the 10 or jack from East. Most players, on the next round, will rest their head on their chin and think of this and that while deciding whether to finesse the 9 or go up with the queen. If they go up with the queen and it loses to the king, they will say "Well, East could have had the J-10 just as well as the K-10." But that, as we have seen, is not right. With J-10 originally East might have played the other card; with K-10 or K-J he had no choice.

        Q 7 4 2
        K 9 6 5 3

This is another common situation:—

South leads the 3, West plays the 10, and the queen is headed by the ace. It is not necessary to repeat the argument: on the way back declarer should finesse the 9.

It comes to this: that a defender should be assumed not to have had a choice rather than to have exercised a choice in a particular way. In the 1955 World Championship match the American declarer would have saved an adverse swing had he drawn the right conclusion on the following hand:—

Deal 17

	♠ 10	F - 3 NT
	♡ A 7	4|4
	◇ A K 9 3 2	
	♣ K J 9 7 4	
♠ Q J 5 3		♠ A 9 7 6 2
♡ 10 5		♡ Q J 9 4
◇ J 5		◇ Q 10 7
♣ 10 8 5 3 2		♣ Q
	♠ K 8 4	Q no choice
	♡ K 8 6 3 2	Q 10 choice
	◇ 8 6 4	
	♣ A 6	

Schapiro and I succeeded in making 4 ♡ after a spade lead and continuation. At the other table the American South played in three notrump. It looks as though, after a spade lead and return, he should make nine tricks by way of one spade, two hearts, two diamonds, and four clubs after the drop of ♣ Q on the ace. In practice he went one down because he did not finesse ♣ 9 on the second round. He suspected that East's queen was a false card from Q-10. It might have been, but the way to look at such problems is this: if East had held Q-10 he might have dropped the 10; with the queen alone he could drop only the queen; that makes the queen singleton more likely, even after the greater frequency of a 4—2 division has been taken into account.

The Coin Test

Many readers will find some conclusions in this chapter hard to accept. Believing that the odds change with every card played, they will see no advantage in going back, as it were, to study the *a priori* expectations. To dispel that illusion it may help to make a simple experiment in a medium other than cards.

Suppose that there are five coins, four heads and one tail. They are divided into two piles, three on the left, two on the right. Now you would say that it was 3:2 against the tail's being included in the smaller pile. Now take two coins away from the larger pile, with the proviso that neither of them be the tail. (That is what happens in bridge, where the discarding is selective and a player who has the critical honor, a king or queen, does not play it wantonly.) At this stage there is only one coin on the left and, as before, two on the right; but it remains 3:2 against the tail's being on the right.

3   2
1   2

PART II

AROUND THE TRUMP SUIT

Chapter 4

TIMING AND CONTROL

This chapter is concerned with declarer's play of trumps; when he should lead trumps and how many rounds he should play.

Most problems of this type arise from the need to provide against a bad break. One accepted measure is to lose a trump trick early. We begin with a standard example:

Deal 18

	♠ A Q J 6 4	H - 6 ♡
	♡ A 5 3	
	◇ A 6 4 2	
	♣ 3	

```
              ♠ A Q J 6 4                     H - 6 ♡
              ♡ A 5 3
              ◇ A 6 4 2
              ♣ 3
♠ 7 2                          ♠ 9 8 5
♡ J 10 8 7                     ♡ 9 2
◇ Q 8 5                        ◇ J 10 7 3
♣ K Q 10 4                     ♣ 9 6 5 2
              ♠ K 10 3
              ♡ K Q 6 4
              ◇ K 9
              ♣ A J 8 7
```

Playing in 6 ♡, South wins the first trick with ♣ A. To keep the hand under control and to provide against a 4—2 break in hearts he must duck a round of trumps immediately. Note that it is not good enough to cross to ♡ A and to duck the second round; a trump return by West will leave South a trick short.

This is a more tricky example of the same type of play:—

Deal 19

♠ J 9 4 2
♡ 7 6 5
◇ A J 3
♣ A K J

H - 4 ♠

♠ K 7 6 5
♡ A K Q 9 4
◇ 10 8 2
♣ 7

♠ 3
♡ 10 8 2
◇ 9 7 6 5 4
♣ 8 6 5 3

♠ A Q 10 8
♡ J 3
◇ K Q
♣ Q 10 9 4 2

A trump not early

South plays in 4 ♠ after West made an overcall of 2 ♡. Hearts are led and South ruffs the third round. The only safe continuation is ♠ Q from hand, to be followed by ♠ 10 if the queen is allowed to hold. If West takes his ♠ K on the second round, declarer's ♠ A will take care of any future heart leads. If West holds off twice, South will cash ♠ A and play on clubs.

If South errs by cashing the ♠ A early, West will hold up his king until the third round. Declarer will then have to cut his losses by playing on clubs, allowing West to make a low trump. South will also be in trouble if he tries a spade finesse. Say that he crosses to dummy with a diamond and finesses ♠ Q; West holds off and South may try to recover by leading ♠ 10 from hand; now West goes up with ♠ K and plays a club, leaving South with singleton ♠ A and no safe way of entering dummy to draw West's last trump .

The next hand, from a rubber bridge game in New York, led to skillful play and counter-play around this theme:—

Next page, please.

NEAR   EXPERTS

Near experts are a funny race,
Talk with their hands, fight with their face.

So much their partners they berate
Their own ego to satiate?

In post mortems repeatedly
You'll hear them say, "I don't agree!"

HIRED HAND

Mary hired a master partner
Whose bids were pure as snow.
And everywhere that Mary went,
A hand she'd surely blow.

POINT OF VIEW

When you or I make a misplay,
It's observed a hand we blew.
If an expert chucks the same way,
They say he took a wrong view.

Deal 20   H - 6 ♠

```
                    ♠ 8 7 6
                    ♡ K
                    ◇ A Q 9 8 7 4 2
                    ♣ A 7
  ♠ Q 5 3 2                        ♠ 4
  ♡ J 9 6                          ♡ Q 10 7 5 2
  ◇ J 6 3                          ◇ 10
  ♣ K Q J                          ♣ 10 9 6 5 3 2
                    ♠ A K J 10 9
                    ♡ A 8 4 3
                    ◇ K 5
                    ♣ 8 4
```

Six diamonds would have been easier, but South played in 6 ♠. West led ♣ K, won in dummy; declarer cashed ♡ K, crossed to hand with ♠ A, and discarded a club on ♡ A. Then, to avoid losing control if the spades were 4—1, he led ♠ J.

West decided that if he was being offered a trump trick it could not be healthy to take it, so he played low. South ruffed a club, returned to hand with ◇ K, and led out ♠ K. Then he played on diamonds, and as West had to follow to three rounds South was able to discard his losing hearts before West could ruff.

Timing the Trump Lead

In the examples so far declarer kept control by not releasing his master trumps. Another way to provide against a bad break is to play first on a side suit. Most players know in principle that when the trump situation is delicate it is a mistake to allow an opponent to win the lead and play off a master trump. A good player would not go wrong on the following hand:—

Deal 21   H - 4 ♡

```
                    ♠ 4 3
                    ♡ A K 6 5
                    ◇ K Q J 2
                    ♣ K Q 7
  ♠ K Q J 5 2                      ♠ 10 8 7 6
  ♡ Q J 9 7                        ♡ 2
  ◇ 6 4                            ◇ 10 9 8 7 3
  ♣ A 3                            ♣ 10 5 4
                    ♠ A 9
                    ♡ 10 8 4 3
                    ◇ A 5
                    ♣ J 9 8 6 2
```

South played in 4 ♡ after West had opened 1 ♠ and North had made a takeout double.

Declarer won the spade lead, cashed the top hearts and played three rounds of diamonds, discarding a spade. West did not oblige by ruffing so South led a fourth diamond and again West let it win. That was the end of the declarer's party: West took the first round of clubs, drew two rounds of hearts and made three spade tricks, for 300 down.

South could afford to lose two hearts and a club; his mistake was to give West a chance to draw trumps. After winning the spade he should play one trump only, then take the discard on the third diamond. If West declines to ruff, the next step is to force out ♣ A. West can force the declarer with a spade, but then the other top heart is played and the rest of the hand is under control.

When there are two top cards to force out in a side suit, declarer must be especially careful. The following hand would deceive most players:—

Deal 22

	♠ 6		H - 4 ♠
	♡ A 8		
	◇ 10 7 6 5 4 3		
	♣ Q J 7 2		

♠ 10 9 7 4 2		♠ 3
♡ K Q 10 7		♡ J 9 6 5 4 2
◇ J 8		◇ Q 9 2
♣ A 5		♣ K 8 3

	♠ A K Q J 8 5
	♡ 3
	◇ A K
	♣ 10 9 6 4

South plays in 4 ♠ against a heart lead. It looks safe enough to win with the ace and draw trumps, but observe what happens when the spades are 5—1:

As soon as South discovers the bad break, he plays a club. The defenders punch in hearts and when they win the second club they punch again. That reduces South to one trump fewer than West and South will not enjoy a single club trick. He will go one down, making six spades, two diamonds, and one heart.

A more careful assessment at the beginning of the hand would have suggested that it belonged to the familiar type in which declarer must retain a trump in the short hand to protect himself from a possible force. ✕✕ A club should be led at trick 2; best defence, as before, is a heart continuation. South ruffs and plays a second club; now the defenders can

One trump in short hand

take their ruff in clubs, but dummy's singelton spade is protection against a further heart play.

This is a less spectacular example of the same type of play below.

Deal 23

	♠ K 5	H - 3 ♠
	♡ 6 4 2	
	◇ 10 7 6 4 3	
	♣ J 9 5	

♠ 10 7 4 2		♠ 9 8
♡ A K 10 9 5		♡ Q 8 7 3
◇ Q 8		◇ K J 9 2
♣ A 2		♣ 8 7 4

	♠ A Q J 6 3	
	♡ J	
	◇ A 5	
	♣ K Q 10 6 3	

North-South go to 3 ♠ over the enemy's 3 ♡. South ruffs the second heart lead and plays a spade to king. If he plays a second spade the hand falls apart. He must force out the ♣ A while dummy still has a protective trump. When West wins with ♣ A he plays a third round of hearts and South discards his losing diamond. A fourth heart will do no damage because dummy can ruff.

This section concludes with two examples that exhibit no profound principle of play but are tricky because it is not easy to see at first that a round of trumps would be premature.

Deal 24

	♠ 10 8 7 6 2	R - 5 ◇
	♡ 7 6	
	◇ 9 8 5 2	
	♣ A K	

♠ K 3		♠ A Q J 9 5
♡ J 10 3 2		♡ K Q 9 8 4
◇ J 6 4		◇ —
♣ Q 10 9 5		♣ 8 7 3

	♠ 4	
	♡ A 5	
	◇ A K Q 10 7 3	
	♣ J 6 4 2	

South plays in 5 ◇ after East has opened the bidding with 1 ♠. West opens ♠ K and continues with a second round. South ruffs and lays down ◇ A, on which East shows out. What next ?

What happens next is that South is one down. He takes two top clubs, returns to hand with a diamond and ruffs a club; then back to ♡ A for ruff of the last club. Now the lead is on table, with no trump left. On a heart play East wins and leads a spade, establishing a trick for his partner's ◇ J.

This hand is plainly a lay-down if trumps fall 2—1, so declarer should give a thought to the consequences of a 3—0 division. Once he sees the road-block ahead, it is easy for him to realise that he must take the slight risk of cashing ♣ A-K before leading a round of trumps.

On the next hand a round of trumps is a mistake because it gives opponents an opportunity to play one more trump than is convenient.

Deal 25

```
                     ♠ Q 6                    R - 6 ◇
                     ♡ J 8 7 6 4 3
                     ◇ 9 6 2
                     ♣ A 8
    ♠ K 7 3                              ♠ J 9 8 5 4 2
    ♡ K Q 10                             ♡ A 9 5 2
    ◇ J 5 4 3                            ◇ —
    ♣ Q 9 5                              ♣ J 6 2
                     ♠ A 10
                     ♡ —
                     ◇ A K Q 10 8 7
                     ♣ K 10 7 4 3
```

Playing in 6 ◇, South ruffs the heart lead and plays on clubs. After three rounds of clubs have passed by without an over-ruff, it does not look bad to come back to hand with a diamond—at least, not until East shows out. If South tries to recover by playing a good club in order to discard a spade from dummy, West will go in with ◇ J and play another trump, taking the last diamond off the table and leaving South with a losing spade.

The safe play, after the third round of clubs has been ruffed, is to return to hand with ♠ A and play a fourth club, discarding the losing spade from dummy. West can ruff and play a trump, but there will still be a diamond in dummy to take care of the losing spade.

Chapter 5

PUTTING THE TRUMPS TO WORK

Trumps are valuable coin and if you handle them properly they will perform a number of small miracles. On the following hand South appears to have four natural losers in a contract of 4 ♠, but good technique reduces them to three.

Deal 26.

<pre>
                        ♠ J 9 4 3   R - 4 ♠
                        ♡ 9 5
                        ◇ J 7 4
                        ♣ A 8 6 2
        ♠ Q 10 7   ♠ 5
        ♡ 10 6   ♡ Q J 8 7 4
        ◇ K 9 3   ◇ A Q 8 5
        ♣ K Q 10 4 3   ♣ J 7 5
                        ♠ A K 8 6 2
                        ♡ A K 3 2
                        ◇ 10 6 2
                        ♣ 9
</pre>

West leads ♣ K and at the second trick South must make a critical play: he must take a club ruff in hand. He plays two top trumps and then ace, king and a low heart. It will not avail West to ruff with his master trump, so he discards. Dummy ruffs and leads a club; South ruffs again. Now comes a fourth heart. West has thrown one club already, and if he throws another now dummy's last club will be good. So West discards a diamond and dummy ruffs. West has to follow to the last club and South makes his fifth trump. The defenders are left in possession of the field, but only three cards remain.

The last hand was an unusal *coup en passant* against LHO, with the club threat an additional feature. The next hand is a more orthodox *coup en passant*, but once again the play has to be foreseen from the first trick.

Deal 27

♠ A 2
♡ A 5 3
◇ A K 7 4
♣ A 9 6 5

R - 4 ♠

♠ 7 6 3
♡ K J 9 2
◇ Q 10 5
♣ 10 8 4

♠ K 8 4
♡ Q 10
◇ J 8 6 2
♣ Q J 7 3

♠ Q J 10 9 5
♡ 8 7 6 4
◇ 9 3
♣ K 2

Three notrump would have been the easier contract for North-South but South persisted with his spades, as players will, so the final contract was 4 ♠.

When West led ♠ 7 South judged that ♠ K would be wrong and that he might lose a trump and three hearts if he finessed on the opening lead. He went up with the ace, and played to make all his trumps.

After two top clubs and a club ruff he led a diamond to the king and ruffed a fourth club. Then a diamond to the ace was followed by a diamond ruff. With only one trump left, he played a heart to the ace and led a fourth diamond to make his tenth trick by ruffing.

WHY *YOU* LOSE AT BRIDGE

In cash bridge clubs, through their portals,
Oft pass Simon's four immortals.
If you play for money in clubs,
You have partnered these types of dubs.

You'll know them well if you have read
S. J. Simon's classics instead;
Why You LOSE at Bridge, number one;
Cut for Partners, sequel in fun.   •

Unlucky Expert so dour
Makes his partners turn quite sour.
And Mr. Smug is no delight.
His attitude is rather tight.

Amusing is Futile Willie
Whose reasons are often silly.
Fifty and on the social climb
Is jolly Mrs. Guggenheim.

In the long run does your expense,
With these partners and opponents,
Exceed your gains, for a net loss?
Do such partners give you the toss?

Let's face the facts, for in this pack,
With such players are you a hack?
At duplicate you may lose face
Yet avoid financial disgrace.

These hands that contain the elements of cross-ruff and reverse dummy are often deceptive. The following deal would hardly seem worthy of inclusion were it not that in a multi-team contest, where only expert players were engaged, one declarer after another had a blind spot in the play.

Deal 28 ✳

```
                    ♠ A K 7 3                    R - 4 ♡
                    ♡ 8 4 2
                    ◇ 7 5
                    ♣ A Q 6 4
  ♠ Q 8 2                              ♠ J 10 6 5
  ♡ 9 5                                ♡ K Q J
  ◇ K 10 6 2                           ◇ Q J 8 3
  ♣ J 9 5 3                            ♣ 10 8
                    ♠ 9 4
                    ♡ A 10 7 6 3
                    ◇ A 9 4
                    ♣ K 7 2
```

When North-South succeeded in reaching 4 ♡ the usual lead was a trump. East holds the first trick and returns a trump, taken by ace. What should South do next?

Several declarers made heavy weather of the play. They ducked a diamond, hoping that if the clubs did not break there would be a squeeze; but when East drew the last trump there was no way for declarer to come to a tenth trick.

It is a deceptive hand, for the answer to the question: "What should South do after winning ♡ A at trick 2?" is "Claim the contract and put down his cards before he makes a mistake."

Reverse dummy play makes the contract a certainty against any lie of the cards. South takes three rounds of spades, ruffing the third; then across to ♣ Q for a ruff of the fourth spade. Now he plays on clubs, ruffing the fourth round if necessary. If opponents play their good trump at any time during this operation, dummy's ♡ 8 gains in stature and will take care of the third diamond.

Leaving Trumps at Large

To leave defenders in possession of a master trump is normal play. Good players often surprise their followers by leaving a low trump oustanding. This is done on hands where the trumps are working hard, so that if an opponent ruffs the declarer will get the trick back by making his trumps separately. As a rule the play makes no difference, but sometimes when the defender ruffs, he has to concede a trick with his next lead.

Deal 29

♠ A Q J 8 5
♡ 7 5 4 2
♢ —
♣ K J 9 4

L - 5 ♣

♠ 9 4 2
♡ K Q 9 3
♢ Q 10 7 5
♣ 6 2

♠ K 7 3
♡ 10
♢ A J 8 6 3 2
♣ Q 8 5

♠ 10 6
♡ A J 8 6
♢ K 9 4
♣ A 10 7 3

After opening 1 ♣, South finished in 5 ♣. West led ♡ K, and taking the view that East's 10 might be a singleton, South won with ♡ A. He could hardly afford to draw trumps right away, so to the second trick he finessed spades. East won with the king and returned a spade. As East was now marked with a singleton heart, South decided to play him for ♣ Q; South led ♣ J from dummy and let it run.

It seemed to be one of those frustrating hands on which the tricks are there but not the means to make them. Insufficiency of entries makes it impossible to ruff two diamonds, draw the trumps and run the spades.

However, South continued with a low club to the 10 and a diamond ruff. A spade was cashed and this was the position when the fourth spade was led:

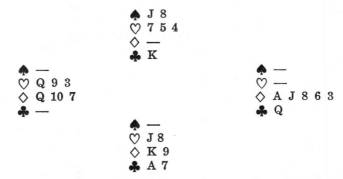

♠ J 8
♡ 7 5 4
♢ —
♣ K

♠ —
♡ Q 9 3
♢ Q 10 7
♣ —

♠ —
♡ —
♢ A J 8 6 3
♣ Q

♠ —
♡ J 8
♢ K 9
♣ A 7

If East discards on the spades, South continues to throw hearts and finishes with a cross-ruff, losing only one more trick. If East ruffs, South discards a heart and East has to play away from ♢ A.

The hand shows that in this type of position it is a mistake to draw the last trump. If the opponent uses it to ruff he may have to return the trick with interest.

Considerations of entry sometimes make it impractical to draw trumps. This happens when dummy has a suit to run but there will be no entry to table if trumps are drawn. Declarer may be able to overcome this difficulty by bringing off what is in effect a trump coup in the middle of the hand.

Deal 30

```
                        ♠ J 3                          Y - 4 ♡
                        ♡ 9 4 3                        coup
                        ◇ J 8 5 4
                        ♣ 9 8 6 4
    ♠ A K Q 10 5                          ♠ 9 7 6 4
    ♡ 2                                   ♡ J 8 6 5
    ◇ 7 6 2                               ◇ 10 9 3
    ♣ 7 5 3 2                             ♣ K Q
                        ♠ 8 2
                        ♡ A K Q 10 7
                        ◇ A K Q
                        ♣ A J 10
```

At rubber game South, playing the Strong Two, opened 2 ♡; and West overcalled 2 ♠. This was passed to South who jumped to 4 ♡, buying the contract. East was chicken to pass on values to raise to 4 ♠. This goes only two down, a profitable sacrifice to kill the heart game that was made. But had East said 4 ♠, or 3 ♠ then later 4 ♠; this deal would never have been published.

West led ♠ K, ♠ Q, then ◇ 7 to South's ace. Things looked dark for South with an entryless dummy, and even darker when West discarded on the second top trump lead. Next South cashed his top diamonds and ♣ A which dropped queen from East, so South exited via another club, leaving:

```
                        ♠ —
                        ♡ 9
                        ◇ J
                        ♣ 9 8
    ♠ Q 10                                 ♠ 9 4
    ♡ —                                    ♡ J 8
    ◇ —                                    ◇ —
    ♣ 7 5                                  ♣ —
                        ♠ —
                        ♡ Q 10 7
                        ◇ —
                        ♣ J
```

Declarer had unearthed a treasure in dummy's trash, the ♡ 9. East returned a spade, the least of evils. South trumped with ♡ 7 to equalize his trump length with East, and dummy over-ruffed with ♡ 9. Dummy led ◇ J to finish East. Frank K. Perkins of Newton, Mass. showed us this over-ruff grand coup play.

The next deal is also difficult, because South has to foresee the ending at an early stage.

Deal 31

	♠ A K 3	U - 4 ♠
	♡ 10 8 5	
	◇ K Q J 10 6	
	♣ Q 3	
♠ Q 6		♠ 10 9 5
♡ K Q J 4		♡ 9 6 3
◇ A 8 7 5		◇ 9 4 2
♣ 10 6 2		♣ K J 9 7
	♠ J 8 7 4 2	
	♡ A 7 2	
	◇ 3	
	♣ A 8 5 4	

South is in 4 ♠ and West leads ♡ K. South wins the second round and leads his singleton diamond. West wins, cashes his heart trick, and leads ♣ 10. Dummy's Queen fetched the king and ace.

South's difficulty now is that even if he can drop ♠ Q in two rounds he cannot draw trumps and finish in dummy to run the diamonds. His most obvious chance is to find one defender with ♠ 10-x-x and ◇ x-x-x-x so that he can draw two trumps, and cash three diamonds.

As the cards lie, this plan appears to fail, but not if South is careful to preserve his ♠ 2 when playing dummy's ♠ A-K. East can trump the fourth diamond lead, but South over-ruffs and plays ♠ 2 to dummy's ♠ 3 to discard his last club on the fifth diamond.

Another occasion on which declarer has to leave trumps at large is when an opponent threatens to take control if another round is played. This is an example from top-class tourament play. See hand on next page.

After a competitive auction in which East-West had bid hearts and North-South the other three suits, South reached 4 ♠ and East judged that he could afford to double, the more so as he read South for a four-card suit.

Deal 32   ♠ J 6 4 2   R - 4 ♠
                        ♡ Q
                        ◇ K J 9 8 5 2
                        ♣ K 6

♠ 5   ♠ A 9 7 3
♡ A K J 7 5 2   ♡ 10 9 8 3
◇ 7 6 3   ◇ A 4
♣ 9 4 3   ♣ 8 5 2

                        ♠ K Q 10 8
                        ♡ 6 4
                        ◇ Q 10
                        ♣ A Q J 10 7

West led ♡ K and, when East played the 10, continued with the ace, forcing dummy to ruff. South played one round of trumps on which East played low. From the double, and from East's encouragement of a heart continuation. South felt sure that East held four trumps. In that case another round of trumps would be fatal, for East would hold off and when he came in with ◇ A would cash ♠ A and force declarer with a heart. After the first round of trumps, therefore, South played on diamonds.

When East won with ◇ ace he had no good lead. He played a heart, dummy ruffed, and good diamonds were played. South had the control and he lost only to the three aces.

Discards in Preparation for a Cross-ruff

The general technique of cross-ruff play is well known, but there is one rare safety move that is worth mentioning. You may need a microscope to pick out South's error on the hand below, but it led to the loss of a vulnerable slam.

Deal 33   ♠ K 7   R - 6 ♣
                        ♡ A K 10 7 2
                        ◇ 6 3
                        ♣ Q J 10 4

♠ A 8 4 3   ♠ Q J 10 6 5 2
♡ 6   ♡ Q J 9 8 4 3
◇ Q 10 8 7   ◇ 4
♣ 8 7 6 2   ♣ —

                        ♠ 9
                        ♡ 5
                        ◇ A K J 9 5 2
                        ♣ A K 9 5 3

South played in 6 ♣ after East had made a pre-emptive overcall in spades and had been supported by his partner.

West opened ♠ A and continued with a second spade. North won and South discarded a diamond. When East showed out on ♣ Q, South turned to diamonds. He ruffed the third round, came back to hand with a trump, and ruffed another diamond. Then he cashed ♡ A and led a second heart; he trumped with ♣ 5 but to his dismay West over-ruffed.

When West led the spade at trick 2, South would have done better to discard his singleton heart instead of a diamond. Then, at the point when he wanted to return to hand after ruffing diamonds twice, he would have been able to lead a heart and trump low without being over-ruffed.

In that example South had to discard the right loser to facilitate entry and to avoid an over-ruff. On the next hand he has to discard the right winner.

Deal 34

                    ♠ K J 4   R - 6 ♣
                    ♡ Q 10 9 6 2
                    ◇ A
                    ♣ A J 10 4
    ♠ A Q 10 7 6 3   ♠ 8 5 2
    ♡ J 8 7 5 3   ♡ 4
    ◇ 7 2   ◇ Q J 10 8 6
    ♣ —   ♣ 9 5 3 2
                    ♠ 9
                    ♡ A K
                    ◇ K 9 5 4 3
                    ♣ K Q 8 7 6

In a pairs event the usual contract was 6 ♣ by South after West had made an overcall of 2 ♠. The play depends on the lead. Suppose, first, that West opens a low heart.

South wins with ace and crosses to dummy with ♣ A; West discards a spade. Placing West with long hearts, South should maneuver to ruff one diamond, draw trumps, cash a diamond and a second heart and exit with ♠ 9; then dummy's ♠ K and ♡ Q will provide discards for two losing diamonds.

If West opens ♠ A and switches to a heart, the play is different. South plays one round of trumps and when West shows out declarer should, as before, read him for long hearts.

The next play must be to discard ♡ K on ♠ K. Then the decks are clear for a cross-ruff. Declarer cashes ◇ A and leads ♡ Q, which East may trump. South over-ruffs, cashes ◇ K, and cross-ruffs the remainder of the hand.

Chapter 6

THE USE OF TRUMPS IN DEFENCE

If trumps are valuable coin for declarer, they are gold for the defenders. In this chapter we shall examine some unexpected ways in which the defenders can take advantage of declarer's shaky trump position.

One well-known maneuver is to refuse to over-ruff at a point when the defender has as many trumps as the declarer.

En Passant Blanc

Deal 35

	♠ K 6 5	R - 6 ♡
	♡ K J 6	
	◇ 9 4 2	
	♣ A K 10 6	

♠ Q J 10 7 3		♠ A 9 8 4 2
♡ 4		♡ 7 5 3 2
◇ J 10 8 7		◇ —
♣ J 7 5		♣ Q 9 8 3

	♠ —	
	♡ A Q 10 9 8	
	◇ A K Q 6 5 3	
	♣ 4 2	

Playing in 6 ♡, declarer ruffed the spade lead, led a trump to the jack and returned a low diamond. East did not ruff, so the queen won. A second heart was led to the king and another diamond was won in hand. Now came a club to the ace, a third diamond to the king, then a low diamond ruffed by the 6. East refused to over-ruff and South could return to hand only by ruffing, which left him with one trump less than East.

South began the play on the right lines but his second round of trumps was a mistake. If he had entered dummy with a club each time he would have retained control.

As the play went, the defence was obvious and most players would have done the right thing. In the next example the critical moment came sooner and it was not so easy to assess the situation.

After North had opened 1 ◇, East made a pre-emptive overcall of 3 ♡. This provoked South into bidding 3 ♠, which was raised to 4 ♠ by North.

Deal 36

♠ K 10
♡ Q 7 4
◇ A 8 6 5 3
♣ A J 4

R - 4 ♠

♠ 9 6 5 2
♡ A 3
◇ K Q 9 7 4
♣ 6 2

♠ J 3
♡ K J 10 9 8 6 2
◇ J 2
♣ K 5

♠ A Q 8 7 4
♡ 5
◇ 10
♣ Q 10 9 8 7 3

The defence began with ace and another heart and South had to ruff. The clubs had to be tackled sooner or later, so South led the 7 and put in the jack. East won with the king and played ♡ K. South trumped with ♠ 8 and West over-ruffed with the 9. That was the end of the defence.

It is clear that if West refuses to over-ruff, the hand goes to pieces. West's defence was that on the bidding he placed South with six spades. As to that, if South had had no worry about the trump suit, he would not have been flirting with the clubs.

When the trumps of a defender are headed by an honor it is still more important for him to keep his powder dry.

Deal 37

♠ Q 7 3 2
♡ J 5
◇ A J 8 5 3
♣ K Q

R - 3 ♡

♠ 10 9
♡ A 8 6 2
◇ Q 10 7 2
♣ 9 5 3

♠ A K J 8 5
♡ 9 3
◇ K 9 4
♣ J 8 7

♠ 6 4
♡ K Q 10 7 4
◇ 6
♣ A 10 6 4 2

South plays in 3 ♡ after East has opened the bidding with 1 ♠. West leads ♠ 10 and on the third round South ruffs with the 7. If West over-ruffs, he will have no futher defence. Instead, he must discard a club or a diamond. South plays ♣ K-Q and leads ♡ J from the table, followed by ♡ 5. West takes the second round and plays a diamond. Now South is on the table and has lost control.

Refusing to Ruff

It is not only when the defenders have a chance to over-ruff that they must cherish their trump holdings. Both sides went wrong on the next deal.

Deal 38

         ♠ A J   R - 4 ♠
         ♡ 10 9 5 2
         ◇ K 10 9 4
         ♣ J 5 2

♠ 6 4 3 2   ♠ 7 5
♡ K 6 4   ♡ A Q J 7 3
◇ A 7 5 2   ◇ Q J 6
♣ Q 8   ♣ 10 9 4

         ♠ K Q 10 9 8
         ♡ 8
         ◇ 8 3
         ♣ A K 7 6 3

South played in 4 ♠ after East had made an overcall in hearts. Hearts were led and continued by the defence, and South had to ruff. He played trumps next, but when East showed out on the third round, prospects were not good. The only hope was to trap opponents into an error. Without drawing the fourth trump South played ♣ A-K and a third club to the jack. West seized the chance to make his low trump, but South was able to return to hand to make his winning clubs and he lost only to ◇ A.

It is clear that if West refrains from ruffing the club, South is badly placed: South is in dummy and cannot return to hand without using his last trump.

South, however, did not play well. If he had foreseen the position, he would have played the top clubs before drawing the second trump. A third club follows, and if West declines to ruff, South can return to hand with a trump.

On the next hand both sides had to decline a Greek gift. (Next page.)

South played in 4 ♠ after East had opened 1 ♡. West began with the ♡ A and dummy ruffed. The lead gave South an opportunity to cross to hand with ♣ A and discard two diamonds from dummy, but as a cross-ruff would hardly produce enough tricks, he finessed ♣ Q instead and allowed West to ruff the ace on the next round. The defence cashed ◇ A-K and East led ♣ K; South ruffed with the jack, led ♠ K, dropping the queen, and a finesse of ♠ 9 left the dummy hand master.

The declarer's play was of a high standard, but West played too quickly when he accepted the offer of a club ruff. The best defence always against this type of unwieldy dummy is to conserve a long trump holding. If ♣ A

is allowed to hold, dummy's clubs are dead. Declarer can still get home if
he plays patiently to establish a trick in diamonds, but that does not
affect the lesson of the hand.

Deal 39

♠ A 9 7 4
♥ —
♦ 10 5
♣ Q J 10 9 6 4 3

R - 4 ♠

♠ 10 5 3 2
♥ A 7 6 2
♦ 8 6 4 3
♣ 8

♠ Q
♥ J 10 8 4 3
♦ A K 7 2
♣ K 7 5

♠ K J 8 6
♥ K Q 9 5
♦ Q J 9
♣ A 2

A defender does not have to have trump length for this type of play to
be effective. The next deal was played in a year when there was a qualify-
ing round for the **Masters Pairs**:

Deal 40

♠ A 7 2
♥ Q J 9 4
♦ A K 8 6 5 3
♣ —

H - 6 ♣

♠ Q 4 3
♥ K 10 8 6 3
♦ Q
♣ Q 5 3 2

♠ J 5
♥ A 7 5 2
♦ J 7
♣ A 9 8 6 4

♠ K 10 9 8 6
♥ —
♦ 10 9 4 2
♣ K J 10 7

Six ♦ was easy, but some North-South pairs bid 6 ♠, trying for the
best match-point score. At one table West led ♣ 2 against 6 ♠

Declarer was awkwardly placed. With six tricks in diamonds and,
assuming a 3—2 break, four in spades, he needed two club ruffs. One
ruff could be taken now, but if he came to hand for a second ruff, the clubs
would be wide open when the trump trick was lost.

South made a good try by leading ♦ A-K. If ♦ K is ruffed by the hand
holding the long trump, declarer can negotiate a second ruff, draw trumps,

and make twelve tricks. However, West refused to fall into the trap. He discarded on ♢ K and declarer had to go one down.

There is one other play that gives South a chance against imperfect defence. Suppose that at trick 2 he leads ♠ 7 from dummy and runs it. West wins and must return a trump, for otherwise South can ruff a club with ♠ A and make twelve tricks with four spades, two ruffs, and six diamonds.

On a final hand of this type the defenders took advantage of inexact play by declarer:

Deal 41

```
                    ♠ A 9 7 6 4 3                      L - 6 ♢
                    ♡ 5
                    ♢ A Q 4
                    ♣ 9 6 5
♠ J 10 5 2                               ♠ 8
♡ A K J 9 6 2                            ♡ Q 10 8 7 4 3
♢ —                                      ♢ J 8 2
♣ K J 2                                  ♣ Q 7 3
                    ♠ K Q
                    ♡ —
                    ♢ K 10 9 7 6 5 3
                    ♣ A 10 8 4
```

After a competitive battle South played in 6 ♢. He ruffed the heart lead with ♢ 5 and led ♢ 6 to queen. When West showed out, South bethought himself, a trick late, of the need to play spades. He played off ♠ K-Q, but East did not come to his rescue by ruffing. This left South an entry short to enjoy dummy's spades and he had to lose two club tricks. His right play at the second trick was to lay down ♢ K, retaining trump entries to dummy in case the spades break badly.

DISTRIBUTION

Lengths and aces, tens and faces,
Distributed in wrong places
Make partners groan, declarers fret,
And make the experts really sweat.

Lengths and aces, tens and faces,
Distributed in right places
Make partners glad, declarers thrill.
But blasé experts just keep still.

VANITY

(A Confidential Conjugation)
I AM a master player,
THOU ART a fair partner,
HE IS a poor duffer.
WE ARE the best partnership,
YOU ARE good steady teammates,

BUT

THEY WON the championship!

Chapter 7

TRUMP TRICKS FROM NOWHERE

This chapter describes some positions in which good play by the defence will win an extra trick in the trump suit itself.

Pursuing one of the themes in the previous chapter, many tricks can be saved by refusing to over-ruff. That it costs West a trick to over-ruff the declarer's queen in a position like this

```
                    7 4 2
   K 9 5                          10 3
                   A Q J 8 6
```

is elementary, but players tend not to recognise that the following position is essentially the same:—

```
                    Q J 4
   10 7                           K 9 5
                   A 8 6 3 2
```

If East accepts an opportunity to over-ruff queen with king his side will not make another trump trick, but if he refuses the over-ruff, he will come to two tricks. It is true that, from East's point of view, he may end up with no trick at all if he refuses to over-ruff and South's trumps are A-10-8; the defender must judge each situation according to circumstances.

It is usually wrong to over-ruff dummy when any length is held.

```
                    J 6
   K                              Q 10 7 4
                   A 9 8 5 3 2
```

If East over-ruffs jack with queen, he will make only the 10 thereafter for declarer's correct play on the next round is ace. If Easts refuses to over-ruff, the defenders will take three trump tricks unless declarer is able to bring off a trump coup.

Refusing to over-ruff may also turn out well as a deceptive play:—

```
                    Q 5
   10 6                           K 9 4
                   A J 8 7 3 2
```

The declarer trumps a side suit with dummy's queen and East discards. South may conclude that the king is with West; if so, he will either play low on the next round of trumps or go up with ace. That will give the defenders a second trick from nowhere.

In a European Championship match between Britain and Italy at Montreux in 1954 Schapiro and I gained a surprise trick from the Italian Eugenio Chiaradia — never an easy feat. This was the trump lay-out near the finish:—

Q

10 5   A J 4

K 9 8 6

At the beginning North had two trumps and declarer six. In the position shown South led a side suit and ruffed with queen; giving no thought to an over-ruff, East discarded another side suit. Declarer came back to hand by ruffing and at trick 11 led the 9 from hand. This went round to East's jack and when East returned the 4 declarer put on the 8 and so lost three trump tricks. It is clear that if East had over-ruffed dummy's queen his side would have made only two trump tricks, for there was no possibility of promotion.

An opportunity for a much rarer coup, based on the entry situation, arose on this deal from Copenhagen in 1948:

Deal 42   R - 4 ♠

♠ 7 4 3
♡ J 3 2
◇ A K 9 4
♣ 9 5 2

♠ —   ♠ K 10 9 6
♡ 9 6 4   ♡ Q 10 8 7 5
◇ 10 7 5 3 2   ◇ Q 8
♣ A K 10 8 6   ♣ 7 3

♠ A Q J 8 5 2
♡ A K
◇ J 6
♣ Q J 4

I was East, playing with the late S. J. Simon, against Norway. When South opened 1 ♠ fourth hand, Simon made one of these shape-showing doubles which he so greatly favored. (Some modern players would instead prefer to make the bicolor notrump overcall to show long minors. Ed.) North bid 1 NT, and over 2 ♡ by East, South bid 4 ♠.

West opened ♣ K and continued with ace and another in response to my echo. I ruffed the third club and exited with a heart. South used his entries to dummy for two trump finesses and made the rest of the tricks without difficulty. (The play was the same at the other table.)

No one made any comment, and it was not until half-way through the next hand that it suddenly came to me: if East discards a diamond on the third club, he makes two trump tricks.

Indirect Promotion

There is many a trick to be won from pushing a side suit through declarer, and the defence should often be so directed. This hand from an international trial was inglorious for East-West, for they passed up a chance of game in notrump to double opponents in a part score and then failed to find the best defence:

Deal 43

	♠ 10 9 7 2	R - 2 ♣ doubled
	♡ K Q 9	
	◇ 5 3 2	
	♣ 8 7 6	

♠ A J 3		♠ Q 8 5 4
♡ A 10 8		♡ 5 4 2
◇ K 10 9 8 4		◇ A Q 7
♣ 10 9		♣ K 4 2

	♠ K 6	
	♡ J 7 6 3	
	◇ J 6	
	♣ A Q J 5 3	

After a pass by South, West opened 1 NT. An 11-point hand normally justifies a raise, but East's hand was so featureless that East thought game would be uphill work. So he passed and, when South reopened with 2 ♣, doubled for penalties.

West opened ◇ 10; East won with queen (better play than the ace) and returned a low spade. South played the king and West the ace. West now continued diamonds, which was the wrong defence. Declarer was able to enter dummy twice in hearts to finesse trumps, and he made five club and three heart tricks.

When West won with ♠ A, he should have continued with ♠ J and ♠ 3. South ruffs and leads a heart; West goes up with ♡ A and puts his partner in with ◇ A. Now a fourth spade from East forces South to lose a trump trick, for he has to ruff with an honor.

The same sort of defence was called for on the next deal.

South played in 4 ♡ after East had opened 1 ♠.

Following the practice affected by some modern players, West opened ♠ 2, the lowest of three. Whatver the merits of that system, designed to distinguish between a doubleton and tripleton lead, it was psychologically bad this time. When East won the first trick with ♠ J, he

Deal 44

	♠ K 10 5		R - 4 ♡
	♡ K Q 10		
	◊ K Q J 3		
	♣ A K 10		

♠ 7 4 2		♠ A Q J 9 6
♡ J 3		♡ A 9 6
◊ 9 6 5		◊ 7 4 2
♣ J 8 7 4 3		♣ 5 2

	♠ 8 3
	♡ 8 7 5 4 2
	◊ A 10 8
	♣ Q 9 6

was too mean to continue with ace and another. The discard on ♠ K was unlikely to help declarer, and when he won with ♡ A East would have been able to play a fourth spade, promoting an extra trump trick.

Below is one more example of long-range promotion that calls for imagination and foresight:

Deal 45

	♠ K		R- 4 ♡ doubled
	♡ 10 9 6 4 3		
	◊ K Q J 5 2		
	♣ 6 4		

♠ A 10 7 4 3		♠ Q 8 6 5 2
♡ A		♡ J 2
◊ 9 6	·	◊ 8 7 4 3
♣ A Q 10 8 5		♣ 9 2

	♠ J 9
	♡ K Q 8 7 5
	◊ A 10
	♣ K J 7 3

South opened 1 ♡ and West, who would have done better to bid one of his suits, made a takeout double. When North jumped to 4 ♡ neither opponent could safely mention his spades and in practice West doubled.

After winning the first trick with ♠ A, West played a neutral defence, cashing ♡ A and exiting with a diamond. He hoped that South would not be able to dispose of his club losers.

This defence would have been good enough had South held only four hearts, together with seven cards in the minor suits. As the cards lay, West could have defeated the contract only by switching to ace and another club at trick 2; when he comes in with ♡ A he plays a third club and East over-ruffs dummy.

Killing Moves

Another well-established reason for persisting with a side suit is to enable partner to kill a winner by ruffing: Two examples follow in which that type of play is easy to miss.

Deal 46

	♠ 8 4	
	♡ Q 10 6 2	
	◇ K 10 7 3	
	♣ Q 10 4	

R - 5 ◇ doubled

♠ 9 5		♠ A K 10 6 3
♡ 8 7 4 3		♡ A K J 9 5
◇ 8		◇ 6 4
♣ K J 9 5 3 2		♣ 8

♠ Q J 7 2
♡ —
◇ A Q J 9 5 2
♣ A 7 6

East dealt at love all and the bidding went:

South	West	North	East
–	–	–	1 ♠
2 ◇	Pass	3 ◇	3 ♡
4 ◇	4 ♡	Pass	Pass
5 ◇	Double	(final bid)	

West opened ♠ 9, and when East won with the king he returned his singleton ♣ 8. It seemed unlikely that East would have led away from ♣ K at this point, so South went up with the ace, drew trumps, and led the second spade from table, establishing two discards for dummy's clubs.

East had thought of playing a heart at trick 2, but the only successful defence never occured to him. He had to continue with a second and third round of spades so that partner could trump and kill one of the discards on ♠ Q-J.

On the next hand the defenders had to continue a side suit in order to kill a menace card.

Deal 47

♠ 2
♡ K 10 7 4
◇ J 7 5 3
♣ A J 6 5

Z - 4 ♠

♠ A 4
♡ Q J 3
◇ A K Q 2
♣ 10 9 7 4

♠ 8 7 3
♡ 9 5 2
◇ 8 6 4
♣ K Q 8 2

♠ K Q J 10 9 6 5
♡ A 8 6
◇ 10 9
♣ 3

South opened 4 ♠ and all passed. West led two top diamonds and switched to a club. The ace went up and trumps were led. After winning with ♠ A, West continued clubs; South played all his spades, and on the last spade West was squeezed in hearts and diamonds.

"I could see it coming," said West, "but there was nothing I could do about it."

It was, indeed, easy to foresee the squeeze. To prevent it, West should have continued with ◇ A, which South would ruff; when West won with ♠ A he would be able to play a fourth diamond killing the jack.

Underhand Play

A defender who holds A-x or A-x-x in trump can always draw two rounds of trumps, but that play has the disadvantage of surrendering control and leaving declarer free to run tricks in a side suit. For this reason it is often better, especially when dummy has a doubleton trump, to underlead the ace.

Deal 48

♠ 7 3
♡ K
◇ A 10 6 5
♣ A K 8 7 4 3

H - 4 ♠

♠ 6 4
♡ Q 10 6 5 2
◇ 7 2
♣ J 10 6 2

♠ A 8
♡ A J 9 7 3
◇ K J 9 8 4
♣ Q

♠ K Q J 10 9 5 2
♡ 8 4
◇ Q 3
♣ 9 5

South's opening bid of 3 ♠ was raised to Four, and East was not so bold as to come in vulnerable at the five level. West opened ◇ 7, declarer played low from dummy, and East won with the king.

Now East had to judge the best return. One possibility was a diamond in hope that West could ruff, but East decided that this was unlikely; for if South had three diamonds, he would be short in clubs and would have played for a discard on dummy's ♣ A-K.

East concluded that the best chance was to win one diamond, one spade, and two heart tricks. A study of the diagram will show that this can be done in only one way. East must return a low spade, leaving the defence with an answer to every attempt by declarer.

That this form of play is a blind spot for the great majority of players was shown when the following hand was included in the 1956 *British Bridge World* simultaneous par contest.

Deal 49   ♠ A J 5 3   H - 3 ♡
                             ♡ K 10
                             ◇ J 4
                             ♣ A Q 10 8 3

♠ K 10 7 4 2   ♠ Q 9 6
♡ 7 4 2   ♡ A 5
◇ 8 5 2   ◇ A K Q 10
♣ J 4   ♣ 7 6 5 2

                             ♠ 8
                             ♡ Q J 9 8 6 3
                             ◇ 9 7 6 3
                             ♣ K 9

South plays in 3 ♡ after East has overcalled in diamonds. East wins the diamond lead and his return at trick 2 is clearly marked once he thinks of it. He must return a low heart so that if South plays for diamond ruffs, the ace of trumps can be played off and the diamond winners cashed. This play does not look difficult on paper, but it was found by scarcely one player in a hundred.

♠ ♡ ◇ ♣ ♠ ♡ ◇ ♣ ♠ ♡ ◇ ♣ ♠ ♡ ◇ ♣ ♠ ♡ ◇ ♣

LITTLE OLD LADY

Hi diddle diddle, the cat and Miss Biddle,
Little Old Lady in slam doubled.
The cozy cat laughed to play such sport,
But Miss Biddle made it untroubled.

PART III

THE FIELD OF TACTICS

Chapter 8

TACTICAL AND NON-TACTICAL FINESSES

When declarer has to choose between a finesse and a play for the drop, his play is often determined by tactical considerations rather than by his estimate of how the cards lie. This often happens in the trump suit when declarer does not mind losing a finesse so long as the trumps are breaking even.

Deal 50

```
                    ♠ K                          S - 4 ♡
                    ♡ Q 7 2
                    ◇ J 7 4 2
                    ♣ K Q 9 6 3
  ♠ 10 8 6 3                        ♠ 9 7 5 2
  ♡ 5                               ♡ A J 9
  ◇ A K 9 5 3                       ◇ Q 10 8 6
  ♣ 10 4 2                          ♣ A J
                    ♠ A Q J 4
                    ♡ K 10 8 6 4 3
                    ◇ —
                    ♣ 8 7 5
```

Playing in 4 ♡, South ruffed the diamond lead and led a low heart to dummy's queen. East won with the ace and returned a diamond. South ruffed, led a spade to the king and returned a heart, going up with the king. A club was led to the table; East won and cashed the good ♡ J. Another club had to be lost and South was one down.

The safety play was to finesse ♡ 10 on the second round of trumps. If it lost to the jack, three clubs in dummy could be thrown on spades and the losing club could be ruffed. South was defeated because he allowed East to draw the third trump.

The next hand is unusual in that declarer must neither finesse for the missing trump honor nor play for the drop; he must play first a side suit, despite the risk of a ruff.

Deal 51   ♠ K 8 4   M - 4 ♠
                                 ♡ A 8 6 2
                                 ◇ A 9 5
                                 ♣ 8 6 3
         ♣ J led
                                 ♠ A 10 9 7 6 3
                                 ♡ K Q 3
                                 ◇ Q 4
                                 ♣ Q 5

South played in 4 ♠ after East had opened 1 ♣.

West led ♣ J, and after ruffing the third club with ♠ 7, South laid down ♠ A, on which East dropped the queen. As we saw in an earlier chapter, the odds favor a finesse in this position, but if South takes a spade finesse now and it loses, East will exit with a heart and South may have to lose a diamond eventually.

Equally it would not be safe to play for the drop in trumps, for if West held J-x-x and the hearts were 4—2, the defence would probably make a trump and a diamond.

The best play, strangely enough, is to lead three rounds of hearts. If the hearts break, they yield a discard for the losing diamond; if East ruffs the third round with ♠ J, he will be on play, forced either to lead away from ◇ K or to concede a ruff and discard.

If West has the doubleton heart, together with the last two spades, he will not ruff the third heart and it may seem at first as if South will be inconveniently placed on the table, wanting to finesse in trumps; but by the simple stratagem of playing the fourth heart and discarding a diamond, he can prepare a way back to his hand.

One further hand that turned on a finesse in trump has no profound instructional point except to illustrate that one must keep one's eye on the ball at this game.

Old bridge players never die;
They just go down with honors.

Deal 52
        ♠ K 8 7
        ♡ A Q 7 6
        ◇ A K Q 10
        ♣ J 6
                                   W - 4 ♠

♠ 6 3
♡ 10 9 4
◇ J 8 5 2
♣ A K 10 7
                                   ♠ Q 10 4
                                   ♡ J 8 5 3
                                   ◇ 9 6
                                   ♣ Q 8 5 2

        ♠ A J 9 5 2
        ♡ K 2
        ◇ 7 4 3
        ♣ 9 4 3

Puzzle: how did South go down in 4 ♠?

West won the first two tricks in clubs and then switched to a heart, won by South. Declarer could afford to lose one more trick and, intent on showing that he knew his safety plays, he led ♠ A and followed with ♠ 2, finessing dummy's 8. This, of course, is the orthodox safety play against Q-10-x-x in either hand. But alas! East won with the 10 and played a third club, forcing ♠ K and leaving his queen in command. If South was going to make this safety play he should at least have played three rounds of hearts, discarding a club, before finessing ♠ 8.

Finessing for Safety in a Side Suit

After the following hand had been played in a match it was presented as a problem to a number of good players:—

Deal 53
        ♠ K J 8
        ♡ A Q 3
        ◇ 7 4 2
        ♣ K Q 9 6
                                     S T - 6 ♣

♠ 10 led
        ♠ —
        ♡ K 10 6 5
        ◇ A Q 6
        ♣ A J 8 7 5 3

South is in 6 ♣, having cue-bid spades. West leads ♠ 10. What is the safest line of play?

Anxious to impress, and misled by the ♠ 8 in dummy, most of the experts gave a rapid analysis: transfer control in spades and play a loser on loser elimination. This means: play ♠ J and ruff East's queen; draw trumps, lead ♠ K to force a cover from East, eliminate hearts and then lead ♠ 8, discarding a low diamond from hand. If, as expected,

West has to win this trick with the 9, he will be on play, forced either to concede a ruff and discard or to lead up to ◇ A-Q.

This is elegant play but as a solution to the hand it is not quite fool-proof. It is not absolutely certain that West has ♠ 9, and also there is just a chance that he has led away from the ace, as South had cue bid a void in spades.

So long as the trumps are 2—1, South can make a certainty of the hand as follows: ruff out the three spades, draw the trumps and play two top hearts, finishing in dummy. That position will be:

```
                    ♠ —
                    ♡ 3
                    ◇ 7 4 2
                    ♣ 9 6


                    ♠ —
                    ♡ K 10
                    ◇ A Q 6
                    ♣ J
```

A low heart is led from North, and if East follows, the 10 is finessed. If West wins with jack, he will be on play. If East shows out on the third heart, declarer plays the king and follows with the 10, allowing West to win with the jack by discarding a diamond from dummy. Once more, West will be on play.

The next hand has a similar point but the analysis is a little more complicated.

Deal 54

```
                    ♠ K J 9 7 5                    P - 6 ♠
                    ♡ A 6
                    ◇ A 10 4 2
                    ♣ 8 3
  ♠ 6                                    ♠ 4 3
  ♡ K J 10 9 4 3                         ♡ 8 7 2
  ◇ 7 5                                  ◇ Q J 8 6
  ♣ Q J 10 2                             ♣ 9 7 5 4
                    ♠ A Q 10 8 2
                    ♡ Q 5
                    ◇ K 9 3
                    ♣ A K 6
```

South played in 6 ♠ after West had made an overcall of 2 ♡. South won the club lead, drew trumps, ruffed the third club, and played ace and another heart. West led a diamond and South played for split honors, but had to lose another trick.

Declarer could have made the contract by playing off ◇ A-K before exiting in hearts, but that would fail if West had three diamonds. The best plan after drawing trumps and eliminating clubs was to play ◇ A and finesse ◇ 9. If West won with a lone honor, he would have to lead a heart away from his king. If West had three diamonds, dummy's fourth diamond would be good for a heart discard. In the unlikely event of West's holding four diamonds, West would be squeezed in the red suits.

Taking an Early Finesse

There are many hands, not easy to classify by type, on which the best way for declarer to keep all the strings in his hand is to take an early finesse in a side suit. The following hand is easy enough so long as declarer makes the right play at trick 2.

Deal 55

	♠ K Q 8 5		W - 6 ♠
	♡ A 8 6 3		
	◇ —		
	♣ A J 7 4 3		

♠ 7 6 2		♠ 4 3
♡ J 9 7		♡ Q 10 4
◇ K J 9 6 3		◇ A 10 7 5 2
♣ 10 5		♣ Q 9 6

	♠ A J 10 9
	♡ K 5 2
	◇ Q 8 4
	♣ K 8 2

South is in 6 ♠ and West makes the inconvenient lead of a trump. If South sets out to ruff his three diamonds, he will run into entry trouble. By the time he has ruffed a third time, he will be left in dummy with only hearts and clubs and no quick entry into his own hand. East will come in with ♣ Q and will cut the liasion by knocking out ♡ A.

The simplest line is to reverse dummy and finesse ♣ J at trick 2. East will win and play a second trump, dummy ruffs a diamond, returns to ♡ K for another diamond ruff, then comes in with ♣ K to draw the last trump and run the clubs.

Since this early finesse is primarily a control and liaison play, declarer does not care if the finesse loses. That point is illustrated in rather striking fashion on the next deal: (*See next page*)

South is in 6 ♣ and West opens a spade. As on the previous hand, declarer needs two ruffs in dummy to make up his twelve tricks, assum-

Deal 56

♠ A
♡ J 10 8
◇ A K J 4 2
♣ A 10 9 5

W - 6 ♣

♠ 7 5
♡ Q 5 4 3 2
◇ 10 8
♣ 7 6 3 2

♠ K J 9 8 4 3
♡ K 7 6
◇ Q 9 5
♣ 4

♠ Q 10 6 2
♡ A 9
◇ 7 6 3
♣ K Q J 8

ing that he is going to make only four diamond tricks. Again there are difficulties over ways and means. If South comes to hand twice in the trump suit in order to ruff spades, he will have to take out ♡ A to regain the lead and draw trumps, and will then be in peril when he comes to the diamond finesse.

The best play at trick 2 is a low diamond from dummy, abandoning the finesse. Whatever is returned, South will be able to ruff his two spades, draw trumps and run diamonds.

In conclusion, here is a hand on which South took one finesse and rightly rejected another:

Deal 57

♠ K J 9 5 3
♡ Q J 10 9 6 2
◇ 6
♣ 10

I - 6 ♣

♠ 10 8
♡ K 4 3
◇ K Q 9 8 4 3
♣ Q 7

♠ Q 6 2
♡ 8 7 5
◇ J 10 7 2
♣ 8 5 3

♠ A 7 4
♡ A
◇ A 5
♣ A K J 9 6 4 2

South was in 6 ♣ and West led ◇ K. There was more than one way to play the hand, but South made as good a shot as any by taking an immediate finesse of ♠ J. East won and led a trump.

South studied this for a while and finally decided that if East had held ♣ Q-x-x he would have returned a diamond to take the trump off the table. Having arrived at that conclusion, South played for the drop in trumps and so landed his contract.

Chapter 9

LOSER-ON-LOSER VARIATIONS

Every advanced book on play has examples of loser-on-loser play and it may be thought that there is not much more to be written on this subject. It is true that in a technical sense there may be no new type to be classified, but within the existing field are many traps and unknown valleys. Thus, one of the most familiar examples of this play is the discard of a loser in preference to an over-ruff that may cost a trump trick. Nevertheless, it is easy to go wrong on a hand like this:—

Deal 58

                    ♠ 7 4
                    ♡ 10 8 5 2   LL - 2 ♠
                    ◇ 10 8
                    ♣ A 10 8 3 2

♠ 10 5 3   ♠ Q 9
♡ A K J 7 3   ♡ 9 4
◇ K 5 2   ◇ A 7 6 4 3
♣ K 6   ♣ J 9 7 4

                    ♠ A K J 8 6 2
                    ♡ Q 6
                    ◇ Q J 9
                    ♣ Q 5

South plays in 2 ♠ after West overcalled 2 ♡. West leads ace, king, then a low heart. If East trumps with ♠ Q, any South player of experience will discard his loser club instead of over-ruffing. But if East trumps the third heart with ♠ 9? Then to over-ruff is equally wrong, but apparently harmless.

Also deceptive in a quiet way, because the loser hardly has the appearance of being a loser, is Deal 59 on the next page.

Deal 59

                    ♠ 10 9 7 4 2   LL - 2 ♠
                    ♡ K J 8 3
                    ◇ J 5
                    ♣ 7 6

♠ 5   ♠ J 6 3
♡ 9 7 6   ♡ Q 10 4
◇ 9 6 4   ◇ A K 7 3 2
♣ K Q 10 9 5 2   ♣ A 3

                    ♠ A K Q 8
                    ♡ A 5 2
                    ◇ Q 10 8
                    ♣ J 8 4

Once again South was in 2 ♠. East overtook his partner's lead of ♣ K, cashed ◇ A-K, and returned ♣ 3. After West had made ♣ 10, a third club was trumped in dummy and over-ruffed by East, and South had still to lose a heart.

The play here was to discard a heart from dummy when West led the third club. The other heart loser could be thrown on ◇ Q, and South would lose only five tricks.

If South had been looking at a diamond loser in dummy at the point when the third club was led, no doubt it would have occured to him to discard a diamond instead of ruffing the club. That is what happened on the next hand, but on this occasion the defence was mistimed.

Deal 60

                    ♠ 10 7 4   LL - 4 ♠
                    ♡ Q
                    ◇ 10 8
                    ♣ A Q J 9 6 4 2

♠ 3   ♠ Q 8
♡ J 9 6 5   ♡ A 10 8 7 3 2
◇ A K Q 7 5 4   ◇ 6 2
♣ 10 7   ♣ 8 5 3

                    ♠ A K J 9 6 5 2
                    ♡ K 4
                    ◇ J 9 3
                    ♣ K

South played in 4 ♠ and the defence began with three top diamonds. It was fairly obvious now that South should discard ♡ Q on the third diamond and not risk being over-ruffed by East. If West had held ♡ A himself, no doubt he would have cashed it before playing the third diamond. As it was, the defence was more difficult. East ought not to have begun an echo on the opening lead; then West might have switched to a heart at trick 2 and the defenders would have made their tricks in the right order.

Preventing Trump Promotion

To prevent opponents from making an extra trick in trump sometimes calls for far-sighted play. South was so gratified, by the opening lead against him on the next deal that he missed a point in the succeeding play.

Deal 61
  ♠ Q J 6 2   K - 4 ♡
  ♡ 7 6 4 3
  ◇ 6
  ♣ K Q 8 7

♠ K 10 9   ♠ A 8 7 3
♡ A J   ♡ K 2
◇ Q J 10 9 2   ◇ 8 7 5
♣ J 5 3   ♣ 10 9 4 2

  ♠ 5 4
  ♡ Q 10 9 8 5
  ◇ A K 4 3
  ♣ A 6

Optimistic bidding landed South in 4 ♡, which would, of course, have been defeated by a spade lead. However, West led ◇ Q, giving declarer a chance. South won with ◇ A and hurriedly discarded a spade on the third club. Then he led a trump from dummy.

West won with jack and put his partner in with a spade; when East played his fourth club, the defenders made their trumps separately, so that even though the trumps were 2—2, South lost a spade and three hearts.

South should have led a fourth club himself and discarded his second spade. Then the defenders would not have been able to make their high trumps separately.

The next hand is similar, but it was perhaps harder to foresee the danger.

Deal 62
  ♠ —   LL - 5 ♡
  ♡ K Q 6 4
  ◇ Q 8 7 4 2
  ♣ Q 7 3 2

♠ K Q J 10 7   ♠ 9 8 5 4 2
♡ 5   ♡ A J
◇ K 9 6   ◇ A 10 5
♣ J 10 6 5   ♣ 9 8 4

  ♠ A 6 3
  ♡ 10 9 8 7 3 2
  ◇ J 3
  ♣ A K

After competitive bidding South became declarer in 5 ♡. West opened
♠ K and South won in hand, discarding a diamond from table. Then he
cashed ♣ A-K, crossed to dummy with a spade ruff, and discarded ♢ 3
on ♣ Q.

This was the critical point of the deal. If South had played a trump now,
East would have won and (if in form) led a low diamond to give his
partner the lead. Then the fourth club from West would have promoted ♡ J.

South avoided this trap by playing a fourth club himself and discarding
his second diamond. West won this trick, but the only other trick for the
defence was ♡ A.

Leaving an Opponent on Play

A most rewarding form of loser-on-loser play is the discard that leaves
a defender on lead with no satisfactory continuation. When the following
hand was played in a match between top-class teams, declarer's mistake
went unnoticed amid congratulations to the defender.

Deal 63

	♠ Q 8 5	E - 5 ♡
	♡ 8 6 4 3	
	♢ J	
	♣ Q J 10 4 2	

♠ 9 7 2		♠ K J 10
♡ 7		♡ 10 9 5
♢ 9 6 4 2		♢ A K Q 10 7 3
♣ 9 8 7 5 3		♣ 6

♠ A 6 4 3
♡ A K Q J 2
♢ 8 5
♣ A K

South opened 2 ♡ (Acol) and defensive bidding by East drove North-
South up to 5 ♡.

West led ♢ 2 and East showed excellent judgement by playing a second
diamond to force dummy. When trumps broke 3—1, South tried the effect
of playing ♣ A-K, but East did not ruff and South had to lose two spade
tricks.

Well as East played, South had a simple answer. When the second diamond was led, he should have discarded a spade from dummy instead of
ruffing. Then he could have entered dummy with the fourth trump and
made eleven tricks.

On the following hand the declarer brings off an attractive loser-on-loser
elimination.

Deal 64　　　　　　　♠ A K 5　　　　　　　　　　X - 6 ♡
　　　　　　　　　　♡ Q 10 8 7 3
　　　　　　　　　　◇ A J 9 6
　　　　　　　　　　♣ J

♠ 9 6 3　　　　　　　　　　　　　♠ Q J 10 8 7 4 2
♡ 4 2　　　　　　　　　　　　　♡ 5
◇ 3　　　　　　　　　　　　　　◇ K Q 7
♣ Q 10 8 7 5 4 2　　　　　　　　♣ 9 6

　　　　　　　　　　♠ —
　　　　　　　　　　♡ A K J 9 6
　　　　　　　　　　◇ 10 8 5 4 2
　　　　　　　　　　♣ A K 3

East opened 3 ♠ and South overcalled with 4 ♡. West passed and North jumped to 6 ♡.

Against any opening lead but a diamond South would have had a simple elimination play. He would have eliminated the side suits and finessed a diamond, leaving East on play.

West opened ◇ 3, however, and declarer had to win with dummy's ace, for the lead looked like a singleton. So he drew trumps and played three rounds of spades, ruffing the third. Then he played two top clubs, followed by a third club on which he discarded another diamond from dummy. West won the trick and had no choice but to lead another club which allowed South to ruff in hand while he discarded the last diamond loser from the table.

DUPLICATE

It was board seventeen
In the Easterns Tourney.
Partner and I had been
Hitting it off pretty.

Partner overbid it
On values insecure.
No one else would game it,
Of that I felt quite sure.

The hand should go down one
In overbid spade game,
Unless rare coup is run
With double squeeze of fame.

Partner played through the quill,
Defenders had no chance.
It gave me a big thrill,
Enough to want to prance.

"Partner! This is joyous!
In play you are no flop.
Your technique should give us
The very biggest top!"

Quickly out the score slip came.
Numbly I stared and sat.
All the scores were the same.
The horrid board was flat!

On the next hand South has more work to do to bring off his end play.

Deal 65

♠ A J 10 6 2
♡ A 10 6 4
◇ J 5
♣ 7 3

X - 4 ♡

♠ 8 5
♡ K 2
◇ K Q 10 9 4
♣ A Q J 9

♠ K Q 9 7 3
♡ 8 7
◇ 6 3
♣ 10 8 4 2

♠ 4
♡ Q J 9 5 3
◇ A 8 7 2
♣ K 6 5

South played in 4 ♡ after West bid diamonds and clubs. At first sight South may seem to have only three losers, one in diamonds and two in clubs, but he has three cards to ruff and after drawing trumps will have only two hearts in dummy. Thus an extra trick has to be found.

West led ◇ K and was allowed to hold the trick. The second diamond was taken by ace and two rounds of hearts cleared trumps. Then came ♠ A and a spade ruff, a diamond ruff and another spade ruff.

Now the position was as follows:

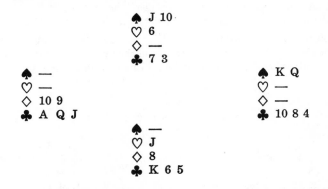

♠ J 10
♡ 6
◇ —
♣ 7 3

♠ —
♡ —
◇ 10 9
♣ A Q J

♠ K Q
♡ —
◇ —
♣ 10 8 4

♠ —
♡ J
◇ 8
♣ K 6 5

Declarer led a fourth diamond and discarded a club from dummy instead of ruffing. West played a fifth diamond and again a club was thrown from the table. Now West had to broach clubs and South's King became good for the tenth trick.

When a Side Suit is Established

Loser-on-loser play is often indicated when declarer has to establish a side suit. The next deal from the 1957 European Championship provoked much discussion:—

Deal 66

♠ A K J 6 4 3
♡ 8 5 2
◇ K J 6
♣ 9

L - 6 ◇

♡ K led

♠ 7 2
♡ A 10
◇ A 9 5 3 2
♣ A Q 8 4

South plays in 6 ◇ against the lead of ♡ K. There is not much doubt that the best way to set about the hand is to win with ♡ A and play two top spades. If not ruffed, and the queen has not appeared, a third spade is led. Now if the queen comes from East, the best play is to throw ♡ 10 and subsequently play West for ◇ Q. If East discards on the third spade lead, South ruffs and follows with ◇ A and ◇ K, playing for a 3-2 break in trumps. If East puts in ◇ 10 on the third spade South discards ♡ 10 as before and takes a view later about ◇ Q.

Although it appears to be clumsy play, it would not be wrong for South to cash ◇ A before playing the top spades. That would, in fact, give him a better chance to make the hand if East had a singleton ◇ Q or ◇ 10.

When declarer is trying to establish a side suit by ruffing, it is sometimes expedient to transfer the ruff to another suit. The next deal comes from the 1956 *British Bridge World* simultaneous par contest:

Deal 67

♠ J 7 2
♡ 4 2
◇ 8 7 6 5 4 2
♣ 6 3

LL - 6 ♠

♠ 4 3
♡ K J 6
◇ K Q J 9
♣ Q 10 7 2

♠ 8 6 5
♡ Q 10 8 7 5 3
◇ 10 3
♣ 9 8

♠ A K Q 10 9
♡ A 9
◇ A
♣ A K J 5 4

South plays 6 ♠ and ◇ K was led. If he trumps a club low, he will be over-ruffed and will lose a heart as well. He can ruff the third round of clubs with ♠ J but must then return to ♡ A and on the fourth club discard a heart from dummy; then a heart can be ruffed with a low trump and the remainder of South's hand will be high. This is not a complicated maneuver, but it defeated most competitors.

A final example combines suit establishment with the earlier theme of preventing the loss of an extra trick in trump.

Deal 68

```
                    ♠ A K 6 4              B - 4 ♠
                    ♡ 2
                    ◇ A 8 6
                    ♣ K 10 7 5 3
   ♠ Q J 3                          ♠ 10
   ♡ A J 8 6                        ♡ K 10 7 5
   ◇ Q 10 7 5                       ◇ K 4 3 2
   ♣ 9 4                           ♣ Q J 8 2
                    ♠ 9 8 7 5 2
                    ♡ Q 9 4 3
                    ◇ J 9
                    ♣ A 6
```

South was in 4 ♠ and West led ◇ 5. Declarer won in dummy, drew one top trump and played clubs. He trumped the third round, but West over-ruffed; then West gave his partner the lead with ◇ K, and another ruff on the fourth round of clubs defeated the contract.

North berated his partner for not drawing two trumps instead of just one. Against good defence, however, that would not have won. West would not over-ruff the third club but would wait to come in with a heart or diamond to play the master trump, and then South would be a trick short.

South's mistake was to ruff the third club. He should have discarded a diamond and so prevented West from making two trumps in addition to a diamond and a heart. Like many loser-on-loser plays, this hand could equally well be classified as a blocking play.

GOOD DEAL

It was gruesome for my twosome;
I was vul. in four spades doubled.
I was sure to endure
A set of five, greatly troubled.
At the finish, it was sinnish,
West held three cards and I had one.
I got off free of penalty;
The misdeal rule was so much fun.

CLOSE BRIDGE HOST

I play old cards, use pencil stubs
On scraps to score. I'm a scrimp slave.
I must admit I'm a dim wit,
But think of the pennies I save!

Chapter 10

HOLD IT!

A sure indication a declarer can have that he is up against top-class opponents is that his attempts to force out their high cards early will meet with failure.

Most defenders recognise the advantage of holding up an ace when they sit over dummy's K-Q, or of holding up a king when they sit over dummy's A-Q-J. Most good players will go further, holding up the ace in the West position when declarer leads from x-x-x in dummy and puts on the king; if this play is made early in a notrump contract it is, of course, most unlikely that the king is unsupported. The object of this section is to persuade players that it pays to be still more daring in similar situations.

Beginners are taught that high cards should be used to kill high cards, but there are many exceptions to that principle. Take this simple and common situation:—

K 6 5

J 10 7   A 8 4

Q 9 3 2

South leads the 2 and puts up the king from dummy. It is not necessary, in practical play, for East to put on the ace. If East plays low, South will duck on the way back and the defenders will still make two tricks. Of course, there may be tactical reasons why East should win the first lead; in the absence of such reasons, it will be better play for the defence to duck and mislead declarer regarding the position of the ace.

Oddly enough, this type of play is equally effective when the defender has A-J-x.

Deal 69   ♠ Q 9 4   D - 3 NT
                         ♡ K Q 6 2
                         ◇ Q 8 5
                         ♣ 8 4 3

♠ A 8 6 2   ♠ 10 5 3
♡ J 8 7 5 3   ♡ 10 4
◇ 10 7   ◇ A J 2
♣ J 10   ♣ Q 9 7 5 2

                         ♠ K J 7
                         ♡ A 9
                         ◇ K 9 6 4 3
                         ♣ A K 6

After 1 ◇-1 ♡ South bids 2 NT and North 3 NT. West makes the lead of ♣ J. South passes to the first trick, wins the second, and leads ◇ 3 to dummy's Q. It is clear that if East wins with the ace, that will be the end of the defence, for after West has shown out on the third round of clubs South will set up the spades and diamonds without letting East on lead.

East can actually hold up his ace on the first round of diamonds with almost no fear of losing a trick. If East plays the 2 and follows with the jack South will play low from hand, playing West for A-x and East for J-10-x. If South's diamonds are headed by the K-10, the defenders are not going to make more than one trick in any event. As the cards lie, then, East will hold the second trick and clear the clubs; South's only chance of game will be to play another round of diamonds and he will finish two down.

There is one combination in which the hold up of the ace represents the only chance for two tricks.

```
                    Q 9 7
        J 10                        A 8 6
                    K 5 4 3 2
```

If South's lead of the 2 is covered by the 10, queen and ace, South's only chance for four tricks will be to play for the drop on the next round; but if East holds up his ace, South will probably duck and lose to jack on the way back.

To hold up a king in the blind position—that is, when sitting over the declarer—is more dangerous than holding up an ace when declarer has played the king. Nevertheless, when at notrump declarer finesses the queen of a suit in which he cannot have great length, it is generally safe to assume that he has A-Q-J.

```
                     5 2
        K 4 3
```

When declarer leads low from table and puts on the queen, the expert game is to hold off. If South has A-Q-J-x, particularly, the hold up will spoil his timing and use of entries.

Holding up a queen is still more hazardous, though this too can be most effective in match-point play.

K J 10 4

9 7 6   Q 8 2

A 5 3

When South, playing notrump, leads low and finesses the 10, it must, in the general way, be good play for East to duck. South will then assume that he has four top tricks in the suit and he may take a second finesse when dummy has no entry or when it is dangerous to allow East into the lead.

Another time for courage is when a doubleton queen is one of the controlling cards in the enemy's long suit.

Deal 70   ♠ J 6   D - 3 NT
                           ♡ K 7 5
                           ◇ 8 4
                           ♣ K J 10 7 4 3
  ♠ 9 7 3   ♠ Q 10 5 2
  ♡ J 8 3   ♡ Q 9 6 2
  ◇ J 9 7 3   ◇ K 10 2
  ♣ A 9 5   ♣ Q 6
                           ♠ A K 8 4
                           ♡ A 10 4
                           ◇ A Q 6 5
                           ♣ 8 2

South was in 3 NT and West led ◇ 3. South won the first trick with ◇ A and led a club to dummy's jack.

Had dummy's clubs been headed by the queen and East held the ace or king, the hold up would have been almost automatic. The queen in this position is the same, in effect, as the ace or king. It must be held up so that declarer can be exhausted of entries to dummy. South will surely finesse again and will be unable to get the clubs going.

Preserving a Vital Entry

A defender who has a long suit and few entry cards must steel himself from the beginning not to let go his entries.

On the next deal South opened 1 NT and was raised to 3 NT. West led ♠ 3 and dummy played low. This was not the moment to finesse against the table, so East went in with the king and returned the 9, and South overtook the queen to win in dummy. The natural play was to attack the

Deal **71**

♠ A J 5
♡ K 6 4 3
◇ 8 5 3
♣ J 10 8

D - 3 NT

♠ 10 8 7 3 2
♡ J 8
◇ K 4
♣ 9 7 6 4

♠ K 9 6
♡ Q 9 7
◇ 9 7 6 2
♣ A 3 2

♠ Q 4
♡ A 10 5 2
◇ A Q J 10
♣ K Q 5

entries of the danger hand, so declarer's first move was to finesse ◇ Q.
West had been expecting this and he played low. South now switched to
clubs; East won with the ace and cleared the spades.

South could have made nine tricks now by playing three rounds of
hearts, but he was not to know who would win the third round and a
repetition of the diamond finesse seemed the best chance. When West won
with ◇ K, he was able to cash two spade winners.

Refusing to Win in a Critical Suit

It is generally good play, in defence, not to win a finesse on the first
round when there is reason to suppose that declarer will repeat the finesse.
A simple example occurs when declarer is induced to repeat an unprofita-
ble finesse in preference to one that would have succeeded.

Deal **72**

♠ 7 5 2
♡ 10 7 6
◇ 9 5 4 2
♣ A Q 4

D - 4 ♠

♠ K 8 6
♡ 9 5 2
◇ A Q 10
♣ J 10 8 5

♠ 9 3
♡ Q 8 4 3
◇ K J 8 7
♣ 9 7 6

♠ A Q J 10 4
♡ A K J
◇ 6 3
♣ K 3 2

Playing in 4 ♠, South wins the club lead on table and finesses ♠ Q.
If West wins, South will subsequently take a heart finesse and make his
contract; but if West plays low, South will probably use his entry to
dummy to repeat the spade finesse and will never have a chance to pick
up ♡ Q.

The next deal is similar in general outlines, but it shows a different way in which the hold up may gain.

Deal 73

                    ♠ 8 5   D - 4 ♠
                    ♡ 10 7 6 2
                    ◇ K Q 8 5
                    ♣ A 6 2

    ♠ K 9 7   ♠ 10 2
    ♡ J 9 5 3   ♡ A 8 4
    ◇ 10 7 4 2   ◇ A J 9
    ♣ J 10   ♣ 9 8 7 5 3

                    ♠ A Q J 6 4 3
                    ♡ K Q
                    ◇ 6 3
                    ♣ K Q 4

Once again South is in 4 ♠ and West leads ♣ J. South wins on the table and finesses ♠ Q, which is allowed to hold. Since East may have ♠ K-10-9, South cannot safely lay down ♠ A and his natural play is to lead a diamond to dummy's queen. East takes with ace and plays a second club. South wins and crosses to ◇ Q for a second spade finesse. Now West takes ♠ K, puts his partner in with ♡ A, and ruffs a club return.

A simple hold up in a side suit on the next hand made a difference of three tricks.

Deal 74

                    ♠ A K 8 7   D - 4 ♡
                    ♡ 7 6 2
                    ◇ 7 5 4
                    ♣ K 6 3

    ♠ Q 10 6 4   ♠ J 9 5
    ♡ 9 8 3   ♡ A 4
    ◇ K 9 3   ◇ 8 6
    ♣ Q 7 5   ♣ A J 10 9 4 2

                    ♠ 3 2
                    ♡ K Q J 10 5
                    ◇ A Q J 10 2
                    ♣ 8

South dealt at game to North-South.

South	West	North	East
1 ♡	Pass	1 ♠	2 ♣
2 ◇	Pass	2 ♡	Pass
3 ♡	Pass	4 ♡ (final bid)	

West made a good start by leading ♣ Q rather than ♣ 5. The old-fashioned lead is much more intelligent when declarer is likely to be short of the suit led. South ruffed the second club, forced out ♡ A, and had to ruff again when East led a third club. Having ruffed twice, South was down to the same number of trumps as West. After drawing these, he crossed to dummy with a spade and finessed ◇ Q. When West played low, South crossed to ♠ A and finessed again in diamonds; now West won with the king and put his partner in with ♠ J to make the rest of the tricks.

It is clear that if West had won the first round of diamonds, that would have been his last trick, as he would have had no way of reaching his partner's hand. South could have made the game, it is true, by continuing with ◇ 10 from hand, but that would have looked foolish if East had held the king.

This was another hand on which a holdup caused declarer to lose control and to go down in a sensational way:—

Deal 75

	♠ K J 4	D - 4 ♠ doubled
	♡ J 7 5	
	◇ A Q 10 8 4 2	
	♣ 9	

♠ 8 6 3		♠ 5 2
♡ A 8 4		♡ K Q 9 6 3 2
◇ J 7		◇ K 3
♣ A Q J 8 7		♣ K 6 2

	♠ A Q 10 9 7	
	♡ 10	
	◇ 9 6 5	
	♣ 10 5 4 3	

In a match in 1950 between a visiting American team and the Lyndhurst Club, South played in 4 ♠ doubled after East-West had bid 4 ♡. West led ♡ A and South ruffed the second round. A finesse of ◇ Q may look like the most natural play, but since South would not be too well placed even if this came off (unless the diamonds were 2—2), South took a deep finesse of the 10.

East could see that prospects would be poor for his side if he gave up diamond control, so he played the 3. Encouraged by this, South drew three rounds of trumps and finessed ◇ Q. Now the roof fell in: East won with the king and collected four tricks, to defeat the contract by 500 points.

If he had suspected the possibility of a holdup by East, South could have played more safely by taking the second diamond finesse after two rounds of trumps only. At worst, East would make a ruff that could be avoided; South would still make his doubled contract, losing one heart, one ruff, and one club.

This is one more hand on which the deadly effect of holdup play is not obvious from a glance at the diagram:

Deal 76

		♠ 9 4	D - 6 ♡
		♡ 9 7 3	
		◇ J 7 4 3	
		♣ A K 8 2	

♠ K 10 6 5		♠ 8 3 2
♡ 4		♡ 10 8 5 2
◇ 10 9 8		◇ Q 6 5 2
♣ J 10 7 4 3		♣ Q 5

	♠ A Q J 7
	♡ A K Q J 6
	◇ A K
	♣ 9 6

Playing the Strong Two, North-South bid as follows:

South	North
2 ♡	3 ♣
3 ♠	4 ♡
6 ♡	

West opened ◇ 10, and after taking one round of trumps, South crossed to ♣ K for a finesse of ♠ Q. Seeing a chance if South could be persuaded to finesse again, West held off.

Ace and another spade would have won the contract now, but South, perceiving no danger, crossed to ♣ A and finessed again. West won and played a third club, on which East discarded his last spade. South was left with a spade loser and no way to dispose of it.

The Holdup with A-x-x of Trumps

A defender who holds A-x-x-x of the trump suit knows that often he must hold up his ace until he can exert pressure against the long trump hand. The advantage, on many occasions, of holding up with A-x-x is not so widely recognised. To begin with, fear that the trumps may be 4—2, when in fact they are 3—3, may cause declarer to make an unnecessary safety play. Below is a simple example in a part score contract:

Deal 77

          ♠ K 8 7   D - 2 ♡
          ♡ Q 9 3
          ◇ J 8 2
          ♣ A Q 6 2

♠ J 10 4   ♠ Q 9 6 3 2
♡ A 8 4   ♡ 7 6 2
◇ A K Q 7 5   ◇ 10 4
♣ J 4   ♣ 9 8 3

          ♠ A 5
          ♡ K J 10 5
          ◇ 9 6 3
          ♣ K 10 7 5

West opened 1 ◇ and after two passes South protected with 1 ♡. North raised to 2 ♡ and all passed.

The defenders began with three top diamonds, and East discarded a club. West switched to ♠ J; South won and played two rounds of trumps, on which West refused to part with his ace. It was now slightly dangerous for South, playing in 2 ♡, to lead another round of trumps, for if West had A-x left, together with his two diamonds, he would be good for three more tricks. Thus the safe play for declarer is to abandon trumps and to push clubs, allowing East to make his low trump. In this example only an overtrick was at stake, but in pairs contests overtricks can be decisive.

When a defender can force a declarer with four trumps to ruff, the holdup with A-x-x can win extra tricks without the element of deception.

BRIDGE PESTS

I hate the drib who tells a fib
On his opening bidding.

You cannot tell so very well
If he is strong or kidding.

I hate the dub who's bound to flub
His dummy hand in play.

And on defense he is so dense
In finding the winning way.

I hate the guy who's out to buy
The bid at any price.

As enemy he's fun to see;
As partner he's not nice.

I hate the whine, "Why'ncha decline
To lead clubs, you rummy?"

Your play was right, but his insight
Was so double dummy.

But the worst pest tugs at your vest;
Recants a hand he played.

He misquotes spots and muddles plots
'til my patience is frayed.

DOUBLE TROUBLE

South opened two notrump
And North next made it four.
Seven notrump South jump bid;
They had the tricks galore.

West doubled, North redoubled;
It sounded like an odd stack.
By mistake some dimwit had
Dealt out a pinochle pack!

Deal 78

```
               ♠ K 5 4                          H - 4 ♡
               ♡ J 10 3
               ◇ K 7 3
               ♣ A 8 4 3
 ♠ Q J 9                          ♠ A 10 8 7 3
 ♡ 8 7 2                          ♡ A 6 4
 ◇ 10 5                           ◇ 9 8 4
 ♣ J 10 6 5 2                     ♣ Q 7
               ♠ 6 2
               ♡ K Q 9 5
               ◇ A Q J 6 2
               ♣ K 9
```

After two passes South opened 1 ♡. North responded 2 NT and over South's 3 ◇ gave preference to 3 ♡. South decided on 4 ♡, aware that he would have to struggle with seven trumps.

West opened ♠ Q and declarer had to ruff the third round. East took the second round of trumps and played a club. When the trumps broke 3—3, the hand was over.

If East had realised that South might have a four-card suit and had held up his ace for another round, declarer would have been badly placed. His only chance for the contract would have been to play another round of hearts, hoping that hearts were 3—3 and that the player who held the ace would have no spade left; as the cards lay, that would have resulted in two down. South could play for one down by leading diamonds and allowing West to ruff the third round.

This type of play will also succeed when the player who holds the ace of trumps is the one who is short in the declarer's second suit. Change the cards a little from the last diagram, and we have:

Deal 79

```
               ♠ K 5 4                          H - 4 ♡
               ♡ 8 6 2
               ◇ K 7 2
               ♣ A 8 4 3
 ♠ Q J 9 3                        ♠ A 10 8 7
 ♡ A 7 5                          ♡ 9 4 3
 ◇ 10 4                           ◇ 9 8 3
 ♣ J 10 6 5                       ♣ Q 7 2
               ♠ 6 2
               ♡ K Q J 10
               ◇ A Q J 6 5
               ♣ K 9
```

Once again South, attempting 4 ♡, has to ruff the third round of spades. He plays hearts and will have no difficulty if West can be persuaded to take the first or second round; but West holds up and South, to have any chance of the contract, must turn to diamonds. On the third round of diamonds West does not ruff but discards a club; then South cannot avoid the loss of a heart and a spade or of two heart tricks.

Another time when the ace of trumps must be held up, but only for one round, is when the declarer wants to draw precisely two rounds of trumps before setting out to ruff his side suit.

Playing the next deal in 6 ♠, South wins the diamond lead on table and leads a trump to the king. If West wins this trick and leads a heart, South will win with ♡ A, ruff a club, return to hand with a spade, and ruff a second club with impunity.

Deal 80

```
                    ♠ 7 6 5 2                         H - 6 ♠
                    ♡ J 6 5
                    ◇ A K 8 4 3
                    ♣ 7
   ♠ A 8 4                              ♠ 10 3
   ♡ Q 9 3                              ♡ K 10 7 4 2
   ◇ J 10 9                             ◇ Q 7 6 2
   ♣ Q 10 5 2                           ♣ J 6
                    ♠ K Q J 9
                    ♡ A 8
                    ◇ 5
                    ♣ A K 9 8 4 3
```

By holding off the first round of trumps West keeps the reins in his hands. If South plays a second trump, West can go in with ace and play a third round, and if South tries to set up the clubs without playing a second trump he will be over-ruffed by East.

Control in the Side Suit

The next deal created much interest for the defence played by Boris Schapiro and myself in the Masters Pairs. It has appeared in several bridge anthologies. (*See deal on next page.*)

After showing long diamonds South played in 4 ♠. Hearts were led and South had to ruff the third round. He followed with the ◇ K and West ducked! To have played the ace would have surrendered all chance

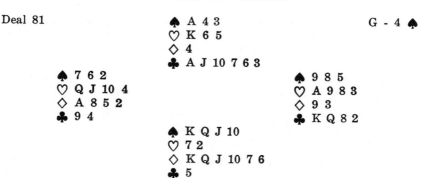

Deal 81   G - 4 ♠

```
                    ♠ A 4 3
                    ♡ K 6 5
                    ◇ 4
                    ♣ A J 10 7 6 3
     ♠ 7 6 2                          ♠ 9 8 5
     ♡ Q J 10 4                       ♡ A 9 8 3
     ◇ A 8 5 2                        ◇ 9 3
     ♣ 9 4                            ♣ K Q 8 2
                    ♠ K Q J 10
                    ♡ 7 2
                    ◇ K Q J 10 7 6
                    ♣ 5
```

of beating the hand. South continued diamonds, West ducked again, and a third diamond was ruffed by East. Now East led a fourth heart and, turn and twist as he might, South had to lose another trick.

Since that hand was played, it has been generally recognised that when the declarer's trump position is precarious, a defender must be most reluctant to let go a control in the main side suit. This is another example:

Deal 82   D - 4 ♡

```
                    ♠ 8 7 3
                    ♡ K 6 2
                    ◇ A Q J 9 6 4
                    ♣ 5
     ♠ A K 10 6 4                     ♠ Q J 2
     ♡ 10 7                           ♡ J 9 4
     ◇ 10 3                           ◇ K 8 7 5
     ♣ K 10 7 3                       ♣ Q J 9
                    ♠ 9 5
                    ♡ A Q 8 5 3
                    ◇ 2
                    ♣ A 8 6 4 2
```

South played in 4 ♡ after West had overcalled in spades. After ruffing the third round of spades, South finessed ◇ Q and East won with the king. Thereafter there was no defence.

East should have refused to win the ◇ Q, for such tricks always come back, generally with interest. South would have followed with ◇ A and another diamond which he would trump in the expectation of bringing down the king; but West would over-ruff and the defenders would make at least one more trick.

Even if South were to take the right view on the third diamond, discarding a club instead of trumping, the play would not be over. After West had ruffed ◇ J the position would be:

```
                    ♠ —
                    ♡ K 6 2
                    ◇ 9 6 4
                    ♣ 5
    ♠ 10 6                         ♠ —
    ♡ 10                           ♡ J 9 4
    ◇ —                            ◇ K
    ♣ K 10 7 3                     ♣ Q J 9
                    ♠ —
                    ♡ A Q 8 5
                    ◇ —
                    ♣ A 8 6
```

The most troublesome lead from West is a spade. East discards a club and South ruffs. Now South must play one high trump, then cross-ruff; he could easily go wrong in the end game.

Transfer the four diamonds of the last example to West, and another startling effect will be seen as follows:

Deal 83

```
                    ♠ 8 7 3                    H - 4 ♡
                    ♡ K J 3
                    ◇ A Q J 9 6 4
                    ♣ 5
    ♠ A K 10 6                     ♠ Q J 4 2
    ♡ 8 5 2                        ♡ 10 9 7
    ◇ K 8 7 5                      ◇ 3 2
    ♣ K 10                         ♣ Q J 9 7
                    ♠ 9 5
                    ♡ A Q 6 4
                    ◇ 10
                    ♣ A 8 6 4 3 2
```

South is in 4 ♡ with a similar type of hand, but only seven trumps. He ruffs the third round of spades and, as his diamonds are solid except for the king, leads ◇ 10 to ◇ A and returns the queen, discarding a club. If West puts on the king, South plays for a 3—3 break in trumps and makes the rest of the tricks. West allows ◇ Q to hold; East ruffs the next round of diamonds and for declarer the hand slips out of control.

He can attempt a cross-ruff, but that fails when East ruffs the third and fourth rounds of diamonds with ♡ 9 and ♡ 10.

Chapter 11

WAITING MOVES

A waiting move is one of the commonest stratagems in chess. A player preserves the balance of a position so that he is able to counter any positive move by his opponent. In bridge this form of tactics is rare but subtle. The following deal created much interest when it first appeared:—

Deal 84

	♠ K Q 3	H - 6 ◇
	♡ Q J 6 2	
	◇ Q 10 9	
	♣ A 4 3	

♠ 9 7 4 2		♠ A J 10 8 6 5
♡ 7 5 3		♡ A 10 9 8
◇ 5 3 2		◇ 4
♣ Q J 7		♣ 10 5

	♠ —	
	♡ K 4	
	◇ A K J 8 7 6	
	♣ K 9 8 6 2	

South plays in 6 ◇ after East has made an overcall in spades. West leads ♠ 2 and the play would normally go as follows:

Dummy's ♠ Q is headed by the ace and South ruffs. After drawing trumps South plays a low heart from the table and East is confronted with a dilemma from which there is no escape. If he goes up with ♡ A, South can discard three losing clubs on ♡ Q-J and ♠ K; while if East ducks the heart lead. South wins with king, discards his second heart on ♠ K, and simply gives up a club.

Now let us improve the defence. When ♠ Q is played from dummy at trick 1, East does not cover. This forces South to make a premature discard on ♠ Q; whether he chooses a heart or a club, the defenders cannot be placed in the same dilemma as in the former sequence.

By the same token South can escape the premature discard by declining to play ♠ Q on the first lead. He plays low from dummy and ruffs the 10. After two rounds of trumps, he leads a low heart from dummy and East has to make a fatal decision, — the ace or the 8; whichever he plays, South has the answer.

The heart situation in the previous deal is often the setting for a waiting move. Compare the spade distribution on the next hand.

Deal 85   ♠ Q 10 7 5   H - 6 ♡
                             ♡ Q 9 6 3
                             ◇ J 7
                             ♣ A 8 3

West	East
♠ A 8 4 3	♠ J 9 2
♡ —	♡ 5 2
◇ Q 10 8	◇ K 6 3 2
♣ K Q J 10 5 2	♣ 9 7 6 4

                             ♠ K 6
                             ♡ A K J 10 8 7 4
                             ◇ A 9 5 4
                             ♣ —

South was declarer in 6 ♡ after West had overcalled in clubs. West led ♣ K and South played low from dummy, taking the ruff in his own hand. After two rounds of trumps he led ♠ 6 and West was in the dilemma: if he played low, South could win and discard ♠ K on ♣ A, and if West played the ace, South would be able to discard three diamonds on ♠ Q-10 and ♣ A.

As on the previous hand, if South goes up with dummy's ♣ A on the first lead, he cannot make his contract, for he has to make a premature discard.

Waiting for Information

The play on the next hand is quite simple, but many players would have had the same blind spot as declarer.

Deal 86   ♠ A K 5 3   X - 4 ♡
                             ♡ A Q 10 8
                             ◇ 9 4
                             ♣ Q 6 3

West	East
♠ J	♠ Q 10 9 7
♡ 7 4	♡ 9 5
◇ K 10 8 6 3	◇ J 7 5 2
♣ A K 9 7 4	♣ 10 8 2

                             ♠ 8 6 4 2
                             ♡ K J 6 3 2
                             ◇ A Q
                             ♣ J 5

South played in 4 ♡ after West had opened 1 ◇. West led ♣ K, and in order to deflect partner from a possibly disastrous switch to diamonds,

East dropped the 8. West continued clubs and on the third round South discarded his obvious loser, the ◇ Q. When it turned out that South had to lose two spade tricks, he was one down.

On the third club South should, of course, have thrown a spade. If the spades were 3—2, he would be able to discard his diamond later. In practice, West would show out on the second round of spades; then South could play ◇ A, followed by ◇ Q, leaving West on play, and not lose any spade trick.

A similar position arose on this hand from the 1957 world championship match between Italy and the U.S.A. :

Deal 87

	♠ A K 7 4	W - 4 ♡
	♡ Q 10 6	
	◇ J 8 3	
	♣ A K 5	

♠ 9 5 2		♠ Q 10 6
♡ J 8		♡ A 5
◇ K 10 4 2		◇ A 7 6
♣ 10 9 8 4		♣ Q 7 6 3 2

	♠ J 8 3
	♡ K 9 7 4 3 2
	◇ Q 9 5
	♣ J

The Italians were satisfied with a part score, but the American South jumped to 3 ♡ over 1 NT and his partner raised to 4 ♡.

West led ♣ 10 and declarer won ♣ A-K, discarding ◇ 5, then ruffed a club and led a heart to the queen. East won and returned a heart. Now South made two right guesses: he went up with ♡ K and then ran ◇ 9 from hand, establishing a discard for his losing spade.

Declarer's idea was to eliminate clubs before leading a trump so that an opponent who won with ♡ A might find himself with no good card of exit. There was something in that, but there was a stronger line that would have enabled him to take advantage of a 3—3 break in spades.

A low heart should be led from table at trick 2. East wins the second heart and plays a club. South must ruff this, for any discard on the ace would be premature. Then he plays ♠ A-K; the queen does not come down, so now he throws ♠ J on ♣ A, ruffs a spade and re-enters dummy with a trump to cash the thirteenth spade.

Ruffing a Winner

It may rarely be necessary to ruff a winner rather than make a premature discard. In a pre-war Olympic contest was this deal:

Deal 88  ♠ Q 10 7 5 3 2   X - 6 ♠
♡ K 9 4
♢ A 9 3
♣ A

♠ K J
♡ Q 10 7
♢ Q 10 8
♣ Q J 10 6 4

♠ —
♡ 5 3 2
♢ 7 4 2
♣ K 9 8 7 5 3 2

♠ A 9 8 6 4
♡ A J 8 6
♢ K J 6 5
♣ —

South is in 6 ♠ and West leads ♣ Q. It cannot help South to discard either a diamond or a heart, and a little study will show that he must ruff the ace of clubs. Then he plays ace and another spade; West must open up one of the red suits and the long card in whichever suit he plays provides a discard from dummy in the other suit.

Preserving a Tenace

In a modest sort of way the simple Bath Coup (holding up with A-J-x when an opponent leads king) is a waiting move. As a general principle of play, a major tenace is of more use in an end game than a minor tenace. That is the lesson of the next deal, which was presented as a problem in the Swedish *Bridgetidningen*. Only North-South cards were shown.

Deal 89   ♠ A J 4   X - 6 ♡
♡ K Q 7 4
♢ A K 8 4
♣ J 2

♠ K Q 10 9 7 3
♡ 9 2
♢ 7
♣ A 10 8 5

♠ 8 6 5 2
♡ 6
♢ 10 9 5 3
♣ Q 9 7 6

♠ —
♡ A J 10 8 5 3
♢ Q J 6 2
♣ K 4 3

South plays in 6 ♡, and West, who has opened the bidding with 1 ♠, leads ♠ K. If South puts up ace and discards a club, he will have to lose two clubs at the finish; but if he keeps ♠ A-J as a rod in pickle for West, he will have a simple end play. After ruffing ♠ K he plays all the hearts and diamonds, finishing in dummy. The last three cards on table are ♠ A-J and ♣ J; if West kept two spades and a club he can be thrown in with ♣ A and forced to lead into the spade tenace.

Chapter **12**

DECEPTIVE MEASURES

Most deceptive plays that can be made in a single suit have been described in *Bridge Play from A to Z* and in other books, and need not be repeated here. Some new ideas have come to light since then, however, and to complete the record I will add some examples of which most arise from articles in the *British Bridge World* by Albert Dormer and myself.

One article studied a group of plays that are an extension of this better known position:

<pre>
            A Q 10 4
J 9 7 5   3
            K 8 6 2
</pre>

When declarer plays a high honor from dummy West must drop his 9 in order to present South with a choice of plays on the next round.

Dormer showed that this type of play can be used in situations where a defender has four cards including 10-8.

<pre>
            A J 7
3   K 10 8 5
            Q 9 6 4 2
</pre>

South leads low and finesses the jack. If East wins with the king, declarer plays ace on the next round. East's best play on the first lead is the 8; then declarer may lead the queen on the next round, partly in the hope of scooping the 10 and partly as a safety play (as he will suppose) against K-10-5-3 in West.

<pre>
            A Q 9 2
10 8 5 3   K
            J 7 6 4
</pre>

South leads low and finesses queen. On this trick West must play the 8 to encourage declarer to lay down the ace next.

<pre>
            K J 7 6
3   A 10 8 4
            Q 9 5 2
</pre>

The principle is the same when the ace and king are exchanged: East must play the 8 when South leads low to the jack.

This is an associated position that was noted in the 1955 World Championship:

A J

Q 10 9 4   2

K 8 7 6 5 3

When South leads the 5, intending to finesse jack, West should go in with the 9 or 10. This may persuade declarer to go up with the ace and return the jack, which would be the right play if West had 10-9 doubleton or a singleton 9 or 10.

Attractive, also, is the deceptive play in the following position:

J 7 5 3

Q 10 9 6   2

A K 8 4

Wanting three tricks from the suit, South plays ace, on which West drops the 9 or 10. South cannot afford then to play the king. His safest play is low from hand, but he may think that he can afford to cross to dummy and lead the jack so as to give himself the chance of an extra trick by scooping the 10-9 doubleton.

The jack play from J-9 is another deceptive move that carries no risk in many positions.

Q 8 5 2

7 6 4   A J 9

K 10 3

When a low card is led from dummy, the jack from East may cause South to win with the king, return the 10, and later finesse the 8.

A Q 8 4 2

J 9   K 6 3

10 7 5

When South leads the 5 West should put up the jack. After the queen has lost the king, declarer may enter dummy in order to finesse the 7, placing East with K-9-6-3.

Tempting a Cover

A later article in the British Bridge World described some situations in which the lead of a high card from dummy might tempt right hand opponent to an indiscreet cover.

9 6 4

Q   J 10 8 3

A K 7 5 2

It costs nothing to lead the 9 from table, and if East is tempted to cover declarer can save a trick by winning with king and ducking the next round.

This type of play is especially effective when East is marked with strength and will therefore be suspicious of any card through him.

10 7 3

K   Q J 9 4

A 8 6 5 2

If this is in the trump suit and East has doubled, he may cover the lead of the 10 from table, not wishing to concede a tempo. Declarer puts on the ace and loses two tricks instead of three.

9 7 5

J   K 10 8 3

A Q 6 4 2

Here again, if East covers the lead of the 9, it will cost the defence a trick.

The same maneuver can be effective when East, marked with some length in the suit, holds the K-10-x or Q-10-x.

J 6 5 2

Q   K 10 8

A 9 7 4 3

Declarer leads the jack from dummy, a play that could cost only if East held the singleton king or queen. East has quite a guess whether or not to cover.

Confidence Tricks

There are many situations in which the defenders may think that they cannot attack a suit without presenting declarer with an extra trick. Very often the boldest action will produce the best results.

Q 10 7

K J 5 4   A 9 2

8 6 3

Suppose that West is defending against 1 NT and can see that he needs four tricks in this suit. Some players will lead the king and follow with the 4, hoping that declarer will put up the queen; others will lead low, hoping that declarer will read them for A-K-x-x. An experienced declarer will generally go with the odds and play West for the jack. Thus the best move, if the entries permit is to lead the jack. This will be covered with the queen and ace and later West will lead low; declarer may go wrong now, convinced that the A-K are on his right.

Still more fruitful of tricks is bold defence in the following position:

J 8 4

Q 10 5   K 7 3 2

A 9 6

If East judges that he must attack the suit, his best play is to lay down the king. Declarers will almost always duck, placing East with Q-10. Defenders often lack enterprise in the following situation:

                    Q 8 3
    10 7 4 2   A J 5
                    K 9 6

If East is on lead and places South with the king, he will generally avoid playing the suit. He should not be nervous about leading the jack. This will run up to the queen, and when East leads a low card later declarer will probably guess wrongly.

The same position is seen from the other side in this diagram:

                    K 9 5
    A 10 6 3   J 8 2
                    Q 7 4

In an emergency West should lead the 10. Declarer may go up with dummy's king, but more likely he will suspect the 10 of being a false card from J-10 and will let it run up to his queen. Next time he is in, West leads a low card and declarer will probably finesse dummy's 9.

Many of the holdup plays described in chapter 10 had a deceptive character, and this is another example of the same kind:

                    Q 6 3
    7   K J 8 4
                    A 10 9 5 2

This is the trump suit and declarer begins by leading low to dummy's queen. Best play for East, on the majority of occasions, will be the 4. The 3 is returned from dummy and East puts on the 8; now South, placing the king on his left, will surely go up with the ace, for it will seem to him that a finesse would lose an unnecessary tempo.

To hold up the king from K-x-x-x is also best in the following position:

                    Q 7
    10 6   K 8 4 2
                    A J 9 5 3

If South's first play is low to the queen, East should duck; then declarer will be disposed to finesse the 9 on the way back.

False Security

While many deceptions are brought about by holding up a controlling card, others depend upon the play of an unnecessarily high card. The following situation has made many appearances in bridge journals, if not at the table:

8 7 2

K J   10 5

A Q 9 6 4 3

This is the trump suit and West has the opportunity to ruff at trick 2. He ruffs with the king and the consequence is that declarer later takes a deep finesse, placing East with J-10-5.

You might play for a lifetime without bringing off that coup, but there is often advantage in ruffing with an unnecessarily high card in order to give declarer the idea that you have no trump left.

Deal 90   ♠ A 5   D - 4 ♡

                                          ♡ 7 4 2

                                          ◇ J 6 4 2

                                          ♣ Q 8 5 3

♠ K J 9 7 4 3   ♠ 10 8 2

♡ Q 8   ♡ 9 5

◇ K 10 7 5   ◇ 9 3

♣ 2   ♣ A J 10 9 6 4

                                     ♠ Q 6

                                     ♡ A K J 10 6 3

                                     ◇ A Q 8

                                     ♣ K 7

With North-South vulnerable the bidding went as follows in a pairs contest:

South	West	North	East
1 ♡	1 ♠	Pass	2 ♣
2 ♡	Pass	3 ♡	Pass
4 ♡	Pass	Pass	Pass

West opened his singleton club and ruffed the club return with the ♡ Q. He exited with a low spade. Although it was not likely that West would have two singletons and not the king of spades, South was sufficiently misled by the play of ♡ Q to reject the spade finesse. He went up with ♠ A and, believing that West was dry of trump, attempted to cash ♣ Q. West ruffed and the contract was one down. If West had held ♡ K-x instead of Q-x he might have effected the same coup by ruffing with the king.

Another way to steal a trump trick is to throw a smoke screen over partner's ability to ruff. Below is a deal from tournament play:

Deal 91

```
                        ♠ K 7                            D - 6 ♡
                        ♡ Q 10 4
                        ◇ K 10 7 6 4 2
                        ♣ A J
     ♠ J 6 5 4 2                              ♠ Q 9 8
     ♡ 9 8 6 3                                ♡ 7
     ◇ 3                                      ◇ A Q J 8 5
     ♣ 9 4 2                                  ♣ 8 7 5 3
                        ♠ A 10 3
                        ♡ A K J 5 2
                        ◇ 9
                        ♣ K Q 10 6
```

North-South bid 6 ♡ and West led ◇ 3. When the dummy went down East could see no hope of beating the contract except by a diamond ruff. To tempt South into possibly careless play, when dummy played low East won with ◇ A and returned the 8. Declarer may have thought the play rather odd but it did not occur to him to ruff high at the possible cost of a trump trick.

Opportunities for play of this kind occur often when declarer is cross-ruffing.

PLENTY TROUBLE

Bridge club partners are a pain,
Cost me money ever again.
Why do partners think I have them
When I sign off to deny them?

Why do partners take me out,
Notrump doubled, so cold no doubt?
Why do partners leave me in
Takeout double, on values thin?

Why quit cold my double, these gents,
On six my trumps and no defense?
Why jump raise by psychic bidding
When they should know I was kidding?

Partners quaver, wrong way bolt,
And give our score a heavy jolt.
Feelings roil, tempers bubble.
All I have is plenty trouble.

Wish I had no cause for bleating.
I must have a towel weeping.
Tonight's game was such a pain,
But I'll be back next week again!

FRUIT SALAD

The Georgia peach, so hard to reach ,
Is a beautiful but bungling dame.
The dry old lemon, a true bridge demon,
Is a bridge expert of well known fame.

The noisy pair who yak and glare
Make many mistakes always the same.
The smooth dead beat is not a treat
If his check you get in a cash game.

Al's tomato is Mae Otto
Whose play is weak, a sin and a shame.
But my friend Anna, a top banana,
Is a Grand Life Master of acclaim!

Playing the next hand in 7 ♠, South had the benefit of a diamond (not a trump) lead. Winning ◇ Q with ◇ A, he set about to cross-ruff. After a club to the ace and a club back, he cashed ◇ K, played ace and another

Deal 92

	♠ K 9 4	D - 7 ♠
	♡ 6	
	◇ 9 7 3 2	
	♣ A Q 10 7 3	

♠ J 7		♠ 6 2
♡ Q 8 5 4		♡ K 9 7 3
◇ Q J 10 5		◇ 8 6 4
♣ 9 6 5		♣ K J 8 2

	♠ A Q 10 8 5 3	
	♡ A J 10 2	
	◇ A K	
	♣ 4	

heart, and led a third club from table. At this point East, who still had two clubs left, went up with the king. It was bold play in a sense, for declarer still had time to draw trumps, finishing in dummy, and make the last two clubs. It was obvious, however, that he was bent on a cross-ruff, and the play of ♣ K would surely encourage him along that path.

As expected, South continued with a heart ruff, a diamond ruff, and then a fourth heart ruffed with ♠ K. This left:

	♠ —	
	♡ —	
	◇ 9	
	♣ Q 10	

♠ J 7		♠ 6 2
♡ —		♡ —
◇ 10		◇ —
♣ —		♣ J

	♠ A Q 10	
	♡ —	
	◇ —	
	♣ —	

Placing the last club on his left, South played the wrong suit from dummy and lost a trick to ♠ J.

If South had been capable of suspecting East's false card, he might have reflected that the last diamond was likely to be with West, for the diamond lead from Q-J-x would not have been very attractive against a grand slam. Thus, an additional feature of the hand is that West did

not play his full part in the defence. He should have played his three
honors in diamonds on the first three rounds, thus making his opening
lead more plausible and also establishing ◇ 9 as a winner in dummy.
That would have seemed to place the fourth diamond with East.

Another strange effect from the play of an unnecessarily high card arose
in the following hand which I defeated in undergraduate days:

Deal 93   ♠ Q 9 6 3   D - 6 ♠
                                 ♡ K J 5
                                 ◇ 9 7 4 2
                                 ♣ J 3

    ♠ J 10 4   ♠ 5
    ♡ Q 8 7 2   ♡ 10 4 3
    ◇ A K J   ◇ 10 8 6 5 3
    ♣ 8 5 4   ♣ Q 9 6 2

                                 ♠ A K 8 7 2
                                 ♡ A 9 6
                                 ◇ Q
                                 ♣ A K 10 7

South was in 6 ♠ and the defence led off with ◇ K, then ◇ A. South
ruffed and played ace, king, then a low club, ruffing on table. As it was
clear that South could ruff a fourth club with impunity, and also that he
had no loser on table, I light-heatedly threw the ♣ Q on the third round.

The effect was quite unforeseen. Having no further loser to ruff, South
played ♠ Q and ♠ A. That left this position:

                                 ♠ 9
                                 ♡ K J 5
                                 ◇ 9 7
                                 ♣ —

    ♠ J   ♠ —
    ♡ Q 8 7 2   ♡ 10 4 3
    ◇ J   ◇ 10 8
    ♣ —   ♣ 9

                                 ♠ K 8
                                 ♡ A 9 6
                                 ◇ —
                                 ♣ 10

East had shown out on the second trump and the play of ♣ Q appeared
to mark the last club with West. Accordingly, South judged that he had
no reason to risk the heart finesse: he led ♣ 10, expecting West to follow
and East to be unable to ruff; instead, West made his jack of spades.

Some of the most artistic deceptions have as their object to prevent declarer from taking a right finesse. East's play on the following hand is simple but effective.

Deal 94

	♠ Q 9 7 3	D - 6 ◇
	♡ K Q J 4	
	◇ Q 9 3	
	♣ K 5	

♠ 4		♠ K 10 8 5 2
♡ 10 8 7 6		♡ 9 5 2
◇ 8 6 5		◇ K 4
♣ Q 9 7 3 2		♣ J 10 8

	♠ A J 6
	♡ A 3
	◇ A J 10 7 2
	♣ A 6 4

South is in 6 ◇ and West leads his singleton spade. As South has opened 2 NT it is obvious to East that he will not enjoy his third-round spade trick. One resource is open to him: to play the king of spades on the first trick in order to make it appear that if there is a singleton anywhere it is in his hand. South may well abandon the trump fiinesse and play ace and another. That will be one down instead of an overtrick.

The opportunity for this type of deception arises often. Whenever the player sitting under declarer has a guarded king or queen of trumps he should look for a play that may deflect declarer form the normal trump finesse. Below is a typical example:

Deal 95

	♠ K 8 4	D - 4 ♠
	♡ K J 10 3	
	◇ 6 2	
	♣ A Q 10 5	

♠ 10 5		♠ Q 6 3
♡ Q 9 7 4		♡ 5 2
◇ K Q 10 3		◇ A J 8 5 4
♣ 8 4 2		♣ K 7 3

	♠ A J 9 7 2
	♡ A 8 6
	◇ 9 7
	♣ J 9 6

Defender against 4 ♠, East overtakes his partner's diamond lead and returns ♡ 2. An innocent declarer may abandon the trump finesse, having the club finesse in reserve should the spade queen not drop.

False Alarm

In the wider field of strategy and control are some clever ways of misleading declarer on the trump distribution. On the following hand West had a certainty of 200 and a faint possibility of 1100, but he wisely made a play that put him strongly in the running for 800.

Deal 96

	♠ 10 8	**D - 4 ♠** doubled
	♡ 8 7 5 2	
	◇ K 6	
	♣ A Q J 8 3	

♠ Q J 6 4		♠ 3 2
♡ A K Q 10 6 4		♡ 9
◇ 9 5		◇ 8 7 4 2
♣ 4		♣ K 10 9 7 5 2

	♠ A K 9 7 5
	♡ J 3
	◇ A Q J 10 3
	♣ 6

At game all the bidding went as follows:

South	West	North	East
—	—	Pass	Pass
1 ♠	2 ♡	3 ♣	Pass
3 ◇	Pass	3 ♠	Pass
4 ♠	Double	(final bid)	

The defence began with three top hearts. East cast two clubs and South ruffed the third round. Since it seemed altogether too dangerous to lead out ace, king, and another spade, South's first idea was to lay down ♠ A-K and then to play diamonds, conceding one down.

On the second round of spades, however, West dropped the jack. South then thought to himself:

"Perhaps West has only three trumps and has doubled on the bidding. Should East, by any chance, have the four trumps, he will not be able to force me with a heart. It looks safe to play a third round of trumps."

Now West was in control and he made, in effect, four heart and two trump tricks. It may seem that West took a risk when he dropped that ♠ J, for if declarer had held six spades and no loser in the minor suits, he would have made the contract. That is true, but as South had been very hesitant about going to 4 ♠ and had laid down the ace and king with a resigned air, West was quite certain that South had only a five-card suit.

One of the most subtle ways of winning an extra trick in trumps occurs when each defender has a trump left and the declarer is afraid to draw them, not knowing that they are divided, evenly.

Deal 97

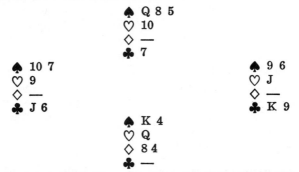

A 5 ◇ bid would have been comfortable, but South played in 4 ♡. West opened ♠ J and declarer won on table. He drew two rounds of hearts with king and ace and played three rounds of diamonds. In response to partner's signal, West switched to clubs and South had to ruff the second round. This left the position shown below.

If South draws ♡ Q, he makes the rest of the tricks. However, he decided to play "safe" by leading a diamond and discardng a club from dummy: someone would ruff, and if another club were led, declarer could ruff on table and return to hand with ♠ K to draw the last trump. While South was working out this maneuver, the defenders had time to prepare a counterstroke. West threw a spade on the diamond lead and East also discarded. Now it looked as if West had the two trumps and had not wanted to ruff in front of dummy's ♡ 10. If so, another diamond had to be played; West might ruff a spade later, but it would be his only trick.

On the last diamond, however, West threw a spade and East ruffed; then came a spade from East and West made ♡ 9 to defeat the contract.

An opportunity for the same sort of defensive play was suggested by the analysis of a hand that was used in the 1956 *British Bridge World* simultaneous par contest, shown below.

Deal 98   ♠ K Q 7   L - 6 ♠
                       ♡ —
                       ◇ J 5 2
                       ♣ A K 9 7 5 3 2

   ♠ J 8 4   ♠ 9
   ♡ A K 7 2   ♡ 10 9 6 5 4 3
   ◇ K 8 6 3   ◇ 10 9 7
   ♣ 10 8   ♣ Q J 6

                   ♠ A 10 6 5 3 2
                   ♡ Q J 8
                   ◇ A Q 4
                   ♣ 4

South had to play 6 ♠, and a heart lead inconveniently shortened the table. The right play for declarer, which by no means readily suggests itself, is to lay down two top clubs and discard a heart, and lead a third club from the dummy. When East follows with the queen, South ruffs with the ace and plays a trump to dummy. Now, with two trumps still against him, he leaves the king in dummy and plays on clubs, discarding his third heart. West can ruff but declarer is in command.

Now change two cards in the defending hands so that the deal appears like this:

Deal 99   ♠ K Q 7   D - 6 ♠
                       ♡ —
                       ◇ J 5 2
                       ♣ A K 9 7 5 3 2

   ♠ J 8   ♠ 9 4
   ♡ A K 7 2   ♡ 10 9 6 5 4 3
   ◇ K 9 8 6 3   ◇ 10 7
   ♣ 10 8   ♣ Q J 6

                   ♠ A 10 6 5 3 2
                   ♡ Q J 8
                   ◇ A Q 4
                   ♣ 4

The declarer follows the same line of play as before, reaching this position on the next page:

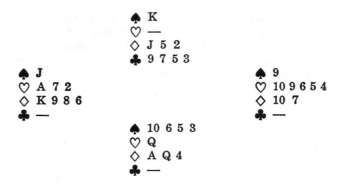

When a good club is led, East discards a diamond and West a heart. If South falls into the trap and plays another club, East discards again; West ruffs and gives his partner a diamond ruff.

This sort of defence calls for co-operation and is not so easy to work out at the table; but the defenders can save themselves thought by relying on the principle that when they are given the opportunity to ruff with a low trump, it is generally better not to do so.

Concealing Wealth

Good players, when playing the dummy, have the habit of turning up in the middle of a hand with high cards that the defenders did not expect them to hold. This effect is achieved by reticent play in suits in which an early trick has to be lost. For example, in this common situation

K J 10 6 5
A 3 2

it is seldom advisable in 3 NT to make the text-book safety play of laying down the ace. The possibility of dropping a singleton queen from East is outweighed by the consideration that should a finesse of the 10 lose to the queen, neither defender will be quite certain who has the ace.

Suppose that South has to broach the following suit:

K 8 7 6 5
Q 4 3

The first play is a low card toward the king, losing to the ace. On the next round, if entries permit, South should play low from both hands. The defenders may be misled as to the position of the queen and may not realise that South has the rest of the tricks.

This is another effective play:

9 6 5 4 2
A K 3

At notrump the best play is a low card from hand.

The principle might have been carried a stage further on the following deal:

Deal 100

♠ A K 3
♡ 7 5 4
◇ 10 6
♣ A K 10 7 2

D - 3 NT

♠ 9 6 2
♡ K 10 8 3
◇ A J 9 5
♣ 8 4

♠ J 10 7 4
♡ J 9
◇ K 7 3
♣ J 9 6 3

♠ Q 8 5
♡ A Q 6 2
◇ Q 8 4 2
♣ Q 5

North dealt and the bidding by North and South was: 1 ♣-1 ◇; 1 ♠-2 NT; 3 NT.

West opened ♡ 3 and South won with the queen. He played top clubs and lost the fourth round to East. West, meanwhile, had had a chance to cast a spade and a heart. This made it clear to East that he had to switch to a low diamond, and the defence took four tricks in that suit to beat the contract.

South would surely have made the game had he led a low club at trick 2 and finessed the 10. That play would have had the double advantage of preventing West from making an informative discard and of making East think that the clubs were twice held, for he would have placed his partner with the queen. It is true that that last consideration would not apply if East's clubs were only J-x-x, but it would still be unnatural play for East to do anything but return his partner's suit.

Discarding in the End-Game

When all is said, intelligent discarding in the end-game, or in preparation for the end-game, saves more tricks than any other form of deceptive play. Good players regard it as an affront to be thrown in at trick 11 and forced to lead up to a major tenace. They prefer, except when attempting a double-cross, to come down to a single honor so that declarer has to guess correctly and play for the drop.

If done early in the play, it is almost always safe to leave high cards unprotected. A good defender who sees that pressure is coming will un-guard his aces, kings and queens before the end-game arrives.

A defender often wants to give the impression that he is squeezed when he is not. This is typical:

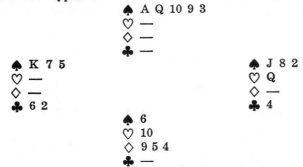

South is playing in notrump and East is known to have the master heart. The only chance for the defence lies in persuading South that East has ♠ K and can be squeezed in spades and hearts.

The question is: what sequence of discards by East is most likely to cause South to go wrong?

Against an opponent who is not especially skillful and will not think about a squeeze until it is in front of his eyes, East should paint the picture in broad colors by discarding ♠ 8, ♣ 4, then ♠ J. In a game of higher standard the best sequence might be ♠ 2, followed by ♠ 8, followed by ♣ 4; that is how a good player might discard if he held ♠ K, so the same sequence may work when he has not.

The play in the last situation depends so much on the human factor that it is difficult to give advice. There is a more precise lesson in the next deal:

PSYCHIC CARD

Al and Charlie were on their way
To Nationals to test their play.

Their car purred o'er vale and ridge
'Til they came to a detour bridge.

The bridge was closed, under repair;
Miles around, hours to get there.

Officer said, "You cannot cross.
"Those are orders straight from my boss."

Al lamented, "We'll be so late.
"They'll fine us points. It's unjust Fate!"

The cop was firm. He would not yield
Despite the way that Al appealed.

Charlie opened his big bill fold,
Membership card, the cop to behold.

Charlie explained, "Experts are we,
"Paid up bridgers. Look here and see!"

"Okay, Boys. Be on your way.
"Cross bridge slowly so it won't sway."

Member's card read so bold and big:
American Contract BRIDGE League!

Deal 101   ♠ A J 3   D - 4 ♠
                        ♡ 9 6 4
                        ◇ J 7 5
                        ♣ K Q 10 5

    ♠ 8 7 5   ♠ 9 2
    ♡ K 10 8 5 3   ♡ Q 7 2
    ◇ 6 2   ◇ A K Q 10 8
    ♣ 9 7 2   ♣ J 6 3

                        ♠ K Q 10 6 4
                        ♡ A J
                        ◇ 9 4 3
                        ♣ A 8 4

South plays in 4 ♠ after East opened 1 ◇ third hand. The defence
takes three diamond tricks and East switches to ♡ 2. South goes up with
the ace and draws trumps, reaching the following position:

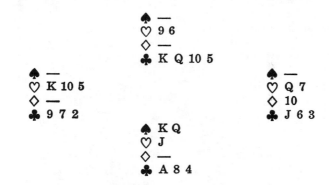

                        ♠ —
                        ♡ 9 6
                        ◇ —
                        ♣ K Q 10 5

    ♠ —   ♠ —
    ♡ K 10 5   ♡ Q 7
    ◇ —   ◇ 10
    ♣ 9 7 2   ♣ J 6 3

                        ♠ K Q
                        ♡ J
                        ◇ —
                        ♣ A 8 4

When the last two spades are led, West must throw ♡ 10 and ♡ K,
putting up the appearance of clutching ♣ J-9-x-x. It may seem that this
would simplify declarer's task if he had ♡ Q; but that is an illusion, for
if South held that card and the king did not appear on the last spade, he
would surely play for the drop in clubs.

PART IV

MATTERS OF TECHNIQUE

Chapter 13

LIAISON AND TRANSPORT

Liaison plays were another subject that has had heavy treatment by bridge writers. Since my last book was written, special attention has been given to the maneuver called avoidance. It is compounded with tempo in the deal below:

Deal 102

	♠ 7 4		T - 3 NT
	♡ K Q 3		
	◇ A Q 10 6 5		
	♣ A 8 2		

♠ J 10 9 6 5 2		♠ K 8 3
♡ 8		♡ A 10 9 4
◇ 8 4 2		◇ K 3
♣ 10 6 4		♣ Q J 9 5

	♠ A Q
	♡ J 7 6 5 2
	◇ J 9 7
	♣ K 7 3

South is in 3 NT after East takeout doubled North's opening 1 ◇ bid.

West lead ♠ J and South wins. If South pushes diamonds, or leads a low heart toward the king, he will make at most eight tricks before opponents run their spades. The correct play, since East is marked with ♡ A, is to cross to dummy with a club and lead a low heart. If East goes up with his ace, it beats the air; and if East plays low, South will win with the jack and shift to diamonds.

By an extension of meaning the term is applied to many situations in which declarer has to prevent the lead from falling into a wrong hand. The critical play often has to be made on the opening lead.

103

Deal 103

♠ K 7 5
♡ J 9 2
◇ J 9 7 3 2
♣ Q 5

T - 4 ♡

♠ A J 10 6 2
♡ 6 4
◇ 10
♣ K 8 6 3 2

♠ 8 4 3
♡ 8 7 3
◇ K Q 8
♣ J 10 9 4

♠ Q 9
♡ A K Q 10 5
◇ A 6 5 4
♣ A 7

South played in 4 ♡ after West had overcalled in spades. When West opened his singleton ◇ 10 South did not reach automatically for dummy's jack. Instead, he played low from dummy and low from his own hand as well. Thereafter he had no difficulty in setting up dummy's fifth diamond for a club discard.

If South covers the opening lead with ◇ J he can be defeated. When East first obtains the lead in diamonds, he will attack clubs and West's king will be established before declarer can use dummy's long diamond.

The next hand is similar in principle but more deceptive:

Deal 104

♠ K Q 5 4
♡ 9 8 5
◇ K 6
♣ A K 7 2

A - 4 ♡

♠ J 10 9 6
♡ A Q 4
◇ J 9 8 5
♣ Q 4

♠ A 7 3 2
♡ 3
◇ Q 10 4 3
♣ J 10 8 5

♠ 8
♡ K J 10 7 6 2
◇ A 7 2
♣ 9 6 3

South was in 4 ♡ and West opened ♠ J. South played the queen from dummy and East won and returned a trump. West played three rounds of hearts and South was left with two potential losers, a diamond and a club. One went away on dummy's ♠ K but there was no way to dispose of the other.

South was left with the task of convincing North that the defence had been good and the lie of the cards unlucky, but that the sun would shine some other day.

South could have made the contract by allowing West's ♠ J to hold the first trick. West cannot effectively play trumps. South can ruff his diamond and establish a club discard by ruffing out East's ♠ A. Clearly, if East overtakes ♠ J at trick 1, he sets up *two* spades for declarer.

Preventing an Unblock

Another use of avoidance play is to prevent an opponent from making an exit or unblocking play. The next deal is from a Gold Cup final.

Deal 105

```
                    ♠ A K 2                        A - 3 NT
                    ♡ 10 5 3
                    ◇ J 10 8 4 3
                    ♣ 8 2
        ♠ Q 9 4                      ♠ J 6 3
        ♡ 6                          ♡ K Q 9 8 7 4 2
        ◇ 9 6 2                      ◇ 7
        ♣ A Q J 10 6 3               ♣ 9 7
                    ♠ 10 8 7 5
                    ♡ A J
                    ◇ A K Q 5
                    ♣ K 5 4
```

East-West vulnerable and East dealt. In room 1 East passed and South, in accordance with his published methods, opened 1 ♠. West passed and North bid 2 ♠. West now re-opened and the final contract was 4 ♣, three down after a killing trump lead.

At the other table I was South and opened 1 ◇. West passed and North bid 3 ◇. East came in with 3 ♡ and I bid 3 NT, which all passed.

Leslie Dodds, West, opened ♡ 6 and the queen was headed by the ace. Not giving the hand sufficient consideration, I played my diamond winners and followed with three rounds of spades, hoping that West would win and would have to lead a club. But West naturally unblocked, so East won the third spade; then, after cashing ♡ K, he led a club through the king and defeated the contract.

This was good defence, but bad dummy play also. A double avoidance play was available in spades. At trick 2 I should have led a spade to the king; then back to ◇ A and another spade. This makes it impossible for West to unblock. If he goes up with the queen, he is allowed to hold the trick and the thirteenth spade wins the contract.

Another point to note is that after South has made ♠ A-K he must not run off all the diamonds lest West jettison the ♠ Q.

Second Hand High

While on this hand it would not have helped West to go up with ♠ Q, second hand high is often a complete answer to avoidance play. West had to take the blame for failing to defeat 4 ♠ on the following hand, though it is true that not many players would have done better.

Deal 106   ♠ K 10 9   U - 4 ♠
                         ♡ 8 6 4
                         ◇ A Q 7 2
                         ♣ Q 8 2

♠ 6 4   ♠ 5 2
♡ K 10 7   ♡ J 9 5 3 2
◇ K 3   ◇ J 10 8 4
♣ A K 9 7 5 3   ♣ J 6

                        ♠ A Q J 8 7 3
                        ♡ A Q
                        ◇ 9 6 5
                        ♣ 10 4

South played in 4 ♠ after West had overcalled in clubs.

West led ♣ K and continued the suit to kill dummy's queen. South over-ruffed the third round and at once finessed the ◇ Q. Two rounds of trumps followed and a low diamond. West played the king and was allowed to hold the trick. Now, whatever West led, declarer was home: a club would allow a ruff and discard and a heart would be up to the A-Q.

It is not difficult to see that West could have avoided the endplay by going up with ◇ K on the first round of the suit. That play would be a mistake if declarer had ◇ J-x and two losers in hearts, but there were many more situations in which the unblock would be necessary.

West might have gone up with ◇ K in accordance with the defensive principle that a high card which must fall on the next round should generally be played at once. The best defence was more difficult to find on the following hand, another example of this type of avoidance play and the defence thereto:

Deal 107   ♠ 7 3   A - 4 ♡
                         ♡ K 8 5 4
                         ◇ A K 7
                         ♣ J 6 5 3

♠ Q J 9 8 2   ♠ K 10
♡ A 6 2   ♡ 3
◇ Q 10 2   ◇ J 9 6 5 4
♣ K 9   ♣ Q 10 8 7 4

                        ♠ A 6 5 4
                        ♡ Q J 10 9 7
                        ◇ 8 3
                        ♣ A 2

South was in 4 ♡ and West, with his all-round hand, made the good
lead of ace, then low in hearts. South won and played ace and another
spade; East won with the king and led a club; South put on the ace,
ruffed a spade, returned to hand on the third round of diamonds and
ruffed his last spade. That made ten tricks—four hearts, two ruffs, and
four top tricks in the side suits.

"Pity I couldn't put you in to lead a third trump," remarked East.

"Pity you didn't unblock by dropping the king of spades under the ace,"
replied his partner. "I would have won the next round and played another
trump."

That ended the discussion, but there were two other "pities" that might
have been mentioned. South should have won the second trick in dummy
and led a spade from the table: if East goes up with the king, South ducks.
Finally, East could have been the bright one by throwing ♠ K on the
second heart lead — a play that could scarcely lose.

A Defensive Counter

Another time when second hand must play high is when declarer is
planning a duck into the other hand.

There was a fine example of this play in the Australian World Olympic
contest in 1950:

Deal 108
           ♠ 10 8 3 2
           ♡ Q 6
           ◇ A K 9 5 4
           ♣ J 10
                                           A - 3 NT

♠ Q 6 4   ♠ J 9 7
♡ 10 9   ♡ J 8 5 3
◇ J 7 2   ◇ Q 10 6
♣ A Q 9 7 5   ♣ 6 4 3

           ♠ A K 5
           ♡ A K 7 4 2
           ◇ 8 3
           ♣ K 8 2

The directed contract was 3 NT by South. West's lead of ♣ 7 is won
in dummy and declarer plays ♡ Q followed by ♡ 6, intending to duck
into West's hand. Having seen his partner's 9 fall on the first round, East
must go up with ♡ J, and thereafter careful defence beats the contract.

Defence against Elimination Play

The same type of play can often be used to prevent declarer from bringing off an elimination. In a *British Bridge World* par contest was a hand
on which a defender with a suit headed by A-Q-J had to open his jaws
like a crocodile and go up with the ace second hand to save his partner

from being left on play with the <u>singleton king</u>. The defence was more difficult on the next deal which declarer played well.

Deal 109

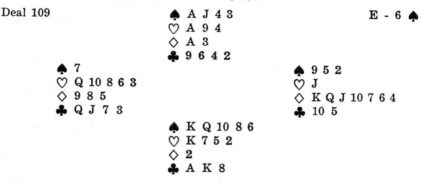

South played in 6 ♠ after East had made a pre-emtive call in diamonds. West led ♢ 9 and dummy won. Prospects were poor, but when East followed to three rounds of trumps, declarer saw a glimmer of hope. He ruffed the second diamond, cashed ♣ A-K, and led a low heart in the following position:

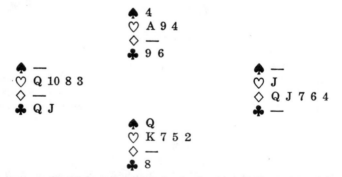

West put up ♡ 10 but South, who had counted East for a singleton, played low from dummy. East had to win and return a diamond; South discarded his club and West was caught in a ruffing squeeze. (South could also have taken the ruff in his own hand.)

If West had kept pace with declarer's thinking, he could have saved the situation by going up with ♡ Q on the lead of low heart. True, that would be a mistake if South's hearts were K-J-x-x: but then his likely play, having found that East was short, would be to lay down the king, hoping to drop the queen or 10.

Skillful Deflection

This play of a high card second in hand is constantly required when declarer is trying to establish a suit without letting one opponent or the other on lead. Many opportunities are missed when a defender is nervous about parting with an unsupported honor.

K 8 4 3

Q 10 7   J 6 2

A 9 5

When declarer leads low from dummy at a time when he cannot allow East into the lead, East must go up with the jack; South will probably abandon the play for an extra trick in the suit.

The same play can often be made when it would cost a trick if declarer knew the true position of the cards.

K 10 4 2

Q 8 3   J 6

A 9 7 5

Once again declarer plays low from dummy and East goes in with the jack. South will win with ace and probably play the king on the next round. If it would cost him his life to let East on lead, South will now abandon this suit and place his trust elsewhere.

A brilliant variation of this coup was described by Alfred P. Sheinwold over twenty years ago:

A 10 8 4 3

Q J 6   9 2

K 7 5

At notrump South has won the first trick in another suit and now cannot let East on lead. He lays down the king and West unblocks with the queen! On the next round West plays the 6 and dummy the ace, and South is afraid to continue.

The same coup can be brought off in the following situation:

Q 10 7 6 4 2

K J 3   9 8

A 5

South leads the ace and West performs a mock unblock with the king.

Preventing an Entry-Finesse

There is another form of second hand high that is not connected with avoidance play. The object is to prevent declarer from gaining an entry by finesse. The defensive play on the following hand will be familiar to good players, but the story of the deal is worth preserving. It occurred in a match between the French and Belgian ladies in the European Championship at Stockholm in 1956.

Deal 110   ♠ J 7 2   B - 6 ♠

                      ♡ A Q J 8

                      ◇ A J 5

                      ♣ Q 5 2

♠ 10 8 3		♠ 9 6
♡ K 10 6 4 3 2		♡ 9 7
◇ Q 8 4		◇ 10 7 6 3 2
♣ 3		♣ A J 9 4

                      ♠ A K Q 5 4

                      ♡ 5

                      ◇ K 9

                      ♣ K 10 8 7 6

The French ladies played the North-South hands in 5 ♠, but the Belgian pair attempted 6 ♠.

As declarer had bid clubs, West opened a heart and not her singleton club. South put up ♡ A and drew three rounds of trumps. Then she led a low club to dummy's queen, and when East produced the ace, her partner could not resist a Gallic gesture of dismay as she realized that a club lead would have defeated the contract.

The by-play was not lost on declarer. Ruffing East's heart return, she led ◇ 9 and finessed dummy's jack! This gave her the necessary entries to take two finesses in clubs through East's J-9-4.

West was still further dismayed when she realised that, after her first gaff she could still have defeated the slam by going up with ◇ Q on the diamond lead to block the second entry to the table.

A little known variation of the play is seen in the following diagram:

                      Q 9 7

      A 10 8 5   K 3 2

                      J 6 4

South leads the 4, intending to finesse dummy's 9; by playing the 10 West can deny South entry to the table.

Creating Entry Trouble

The remainder of this chapter is concerned with one of the most important and least analysed forms of defensive play, the attack on entries before declarer can use them.

To set the mood, we will begin with a fairly spectacular example:

Deal 111
     ♠ A Q 8 4 2   E - 6 ♣
     ♡ A Q 9 8 4
     ◇ J 9 5
     ♣ —

♠ J 9 7   ♠ K 10 5
♡ 7 6   ♡ K J 5 2
◇ Q 10 6 3   ◇ 8 4 2
♣ 10 7 3 2   ♣ 9 6 5

     ♠ 6 3
     ♡ 10 3
     ◇ A K 7
     ♣ A K Q J 8 4

North opened 1 ♠ and South, after discovering that his partner held two aces, forced the bidding up to 6 ♣.

West led ♡ 7 and East won the first trick with jack. He returned a diamond up to weakness, whereupon South drew trumps, led a heart to the ace and played East for ♡ K, making twelve tricks.

East should have foreseen this danger and should have returned a heart at trick 2 to cut liaison. That would have held South to two heart tricks in all and he would have had to lose a spade or a diamond.

Taking Advantage of a Blocked Suit

The point of the defence on the last hand was that East had to return a heart while West had a trump with which to interrupt the run of the suit. More often, the object of such play is to attack an entry before declarer has had an opportunity to unblock one of his suits.

Deal 112
     ♠ 10 5 3 2   E - 4 ♡
     ♡ J
     ◇ J 9 3
     ♣ Q J 10 8 3

♠ K J 4   ♠ 8 7 6
♡ 5 4   ♡ 7 6 3
◇ 10 8 6 5 2   ◇ A 7 4
♣ K 7 4   ♣ A 9 5 2

     ♠ A Q 9
     ♡ A K Q 10 9 8 2
     ◇ K Q
     ♣ 6

South opened with a forcing bid and went to 4 ♡ on his own. West led ◇ 5, and East won with ace, and South dropped the king. When East returned a spade South went up with the ace, cashed ◇ Q, entered dummy with ♡ J and discarded a loser on ◇ J. This gave him ten tricks.

If West's ◇ 5 was to be read as fourth best, East, by deducting 5 from 11, could have worked out that South had two diamonds higher than the 5. These were obviously ◇ K-Q, so the right defence was to return a trump at trick 2, killing dummy's only entry before ◇ J could be enjoyed.

A dry honor combination such as South's ◇ K-Q is the usual sign that declarer may have entry trouble. The defenders recognised this and co-operated to fine effect on the next deal from a match between England and Eire.

Deal 113

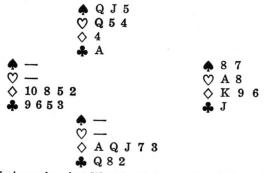

                    ♠ Q J 10 5 2   E - 3 NT
                    ♡ Q 5 4 3 2
                    ◇ 4
                    ♣ A K
    ♠ 9 4   ♠ A 8 7 3
    ♡ K J   ♡ A 8 7 6
    ◇ 10 8 5 2   ◇ K 9 6
    ♣ 9 6 5 4 3   ♣ J 10
                    ♠ K 6
                    ♡ 10 9
                    ◇ A Q J 7 3
                    ♣ Q 8 7 2

The Irish pair reached 3 NT, which looks doubtful on the North-South hands but is not easy to defeat. Declarer won the club lead in dummy and pushed spades, East won the second round. East made a good switch at this point, leading a low heart in preference to a club. West won with ♡ K and played ♡ J, which held the trick. The position was now:

                    ♠ Q J 5
                    ♡ Q 5 4
                    ◇ 4
                    ♣ A
    ♠ —   ♠ 8 7
    ♡ —   ♡ A 8
    ◇ 10 8 5 2   ◇ K 9 6
    ♣ 9 6 5 3   ♣ J
                    ♠ —
                    ♡ —
                    ◇ A Q J 7 3
                    ♣ Q 8 2

A club is the obvious play, but West looked more deeply into the position. He saw that if declarer had ◇ A-Q, together with a club trick, as seemed likely from East's failure to continue the suit, he would have enough tricks for game if a club were played now. Better defence was a diamond, while the ♣ A was still in the way. So West led ◇ 8 and East correctly withheld his king. Declarer made ◇ Q and ◇ A but had to concede two hearts at the finish.

An Attack from Long Range

This is another ordinary-seeming hand on which the defence's opportunity to create entry trouble is seldom noticed:

Deal 114   ♠ 7 5 3   E - 4 ♡
                      ♡ Q 6 4
                      ◇ A J 8 6 5
                      ♣ K 9

   ♠ Q 8 6 2   ♠ J 10 4
   ♡ 10 7   ♡ 5 3
   ◇ 9 4   ◇ K Q 10 3
   ♣ 10 8 6 4 3   ♣ A Q 7 2

                 ♠ A K 9
                 ♡ A K J 9 8 2
                 ◇ 7 2
                 ♣ J 5

West opened ♣ 4 against 4 ♡ and East won the first two tricks. The presence of a long suit in dummy generally suggests the need to attack entries, but the lead of a spade up to dummy's weakness seemed obvious and East switched to ♠ J. South won with ace and ducked a round of diamonds; East played a second spade and the king won. Now South laid down ♡ A, led a diamond to the ace and ruffed a diamond with ♡ J; when trumps broke 2—2 he was able to set up the fifth diamond.

It was not an obvious defence by any means, but East should have returned a trump at trick 3. A count of entries would have shown him that dummy's diamonds could be killed, so there was no hurry to attack spades, South would have won the trump lead and ducked a diamond; then East plays a second trump; this is the killer, for it makes South use an entry to dummy before he has begun to ruff diamonds.

Playing a Passive Game

Another way of upsetting declarer's liaison is by playing dummy's long suit. Apart from the well-known defence at a suit contract where the object of the play is to sever declarer's transport to dummy, there is advantage in playing dummy's suit at notrump before it is convenient for declarer to run his winners.

One obvious occasion for the play is when declarer has only a single entry to dummy and cannot cash winners without setting up tricks for the defence, as in the following diagram:

If the suit is not played early, declarer will be able to cash his three

A K Q 6 3

J 9 5 2   10 8 4

7

tricks when it suits him and the long cards may be useful for a squeeze in the end-game. It will pay the defenders still more to lead the suit if their seven cards are divided 5—2 instead of 4—3.

Most players would see the advantage of attacking this suit if they knew that declarer had a singleton; what they do not realise is that is may well be good tactics to play the suit when declarer has a doubleton and can make all five tricks.

Almost all average players are much too busy in their defence to no-trump contracts. If their first attack does not draw blood, they lunge here and there, all the time opening up suits to declarer's advantage. Good players, jealous of every trick from experience of match point play, are more inclined to let declarer do his own work.

When dummy has a long suit and no side entry, it may be embarrassing for declarer to have to run that suit before he is ready.

Deal 115   ♠ J 7 5   Z - 3 NT

                              ♡ —
                              ◇ A K Q 7 3
                              ♣ Q 7 6 5 2

♠ A 10 2   ♠ Q 8 6 4
♡ K 9 8 4   ♡ J 10 5 3
◇ 10 8 6 2   ◇ 9 4
♣ J 10   ♣ K 9 4

                              ♠ K 9 3
                              ♡ A Q 7 6 2
                              ◇ J 5
                              ♣ A 8 3

South was in 3 NT and West led ♣ J. South won with ace and returned a club, allowing West to hold the trick with the 10. West led a low diamond, won by jack, and a third club went to East's king.

East could see that South had five winners in diamonds and three in clubs. It was too much to hope that the defenders could take three tricks in either hearts or spades, so East played a passive game, returning a diamond to dummy.

This play proved surprisingly effective. South ran off the minor suit winners, but when he came to the last one he was badly placed, for his last four cards were ♠ K-9-3 and ♡ A and he still had a discard to find. As West, with ♡ K and ♠ A-10-2, was over him, South was squeezed and could not take another trick.

Chapter 14

METHODS OF SUIT ESTABLISHMENT

Although every text-book has its list of standard safety plays, some practical ones have escaped attention. Thus it will surprise most players to learn that there is a safety play in such a commonplace situation as:

5

K Q 7 6 4 3 2

If declarer can afford to lose only one trick he must lead from dummy and play East for A-x. But if he can afford to lose two tricks, the first play should be a low card from both hands. This saves a trick when West has the singleton ace.

The combination

3 2

K Q 10 6 5 4

raises so many problems that it may be best to set them out in tabular form.

(a) *South can lead twice from table and can afford to lose two tricks.*
He could go up with queen on the first round, finessing the 10 would lose three tricks if West had singleton jack.

(b) *South can lead twice from table and can afford to lose only one trick.*
Now only the 3—2 distributions have to be considered. Best play is the king on the first round. If it holds, the next lead should be from table and if East plays low again the queen should be played.

This method of play loses when West has A-x and holds off, but it gains when he has J-x. The factor that decides is that it is more difficult for West, holding A-x, to hold off the king (which may be wrong play) than for East to duck twice with A-x-x.

(c) *South can lead once from table and can afford to lose only one trick.*
Now a finesse of the 10 is best. It gains against J-x-x and A-J-x in East. True, it loses when East has A-x and A-x-x, but those two combinations cannot both be counted on the other side, for if South goes up with the king and it holds he will not know whether to return the queen or a low card.

(d) *South can lead once from table and can afford to lose two tricks.*
Again the 10 is best, for it is a losing play only when West has singleton jack. (If South is not already on the table it is equally good to lead the king from hand, then enter dummy and finesse the 10. That loses only to East's singleton ace.)

(e) *As an appendage to the last situation, suppose again that South can lead only once from table and can afford to lose two tricks, but can exclude the possibility of A-J-9-x in East.*

In that case the best play will be low from hand: that will keep down the loss against both singleton jack and singleton ace on the left.

There is a little known safety play with this holding:

6 5 4

K J 10 3 2

Suppose that South can afford to lose two tricks but can lead only from dummy once. He should put up king, for that saves a trick if West has singleton queen. If the 10 is finessed, three tricks are lost against singleton queen and singleton ace.

This is another deceptive combination:

5

A J 10 6 4 2

If declarer needs five tricks he must play East for K-Q-x, but if he can afford to lose two tricks, the ace or a low card first is better. West is more likely (in a ratio of 8 to 6) to have K-x or Q-x than x-x.

The addition of the 8 does not alter the play:

A

J 10 8 6 4 2

After playing the ace declarer should lead low from hand, not the jack. The jack gains if either opponent has 9-x, but it loses both to K-x and Q-x.

With A-Q-10-x-x-x opposite a singleton a finesse of the queen or 10 offers an equal chance for five tricks, though for reasons of control the 10 should usually be preferred; but here the possession of intermediate cards makes a difference:

9

A Q 10 8 4 3

Now the queen should be finessed, for that wins five tricks when West has J-x, whereas finessing the 10 loses two tricks against either K-x or J-x in West.

An extension of some of the safety plays shown above occurs in the following diagram:

J 10 7 4 3

Q 9 8 5   **A 2**

K 6

South plays low from dummy and wins with the king. On the way back he should duck in dummy, for if the suit is 3—3 it does not matter what he does, but if the cards are as shown, then playing the 10 costs an unnecessary trick.

The same play can sometimes be made when the cards are as follows:

<pre>
              Q 10 6 5 3
  K 9 7 4   A 8
              J 2
</pre>

Declarer leads low from dummy and puts on the jack. At notrump West may hold off, placing South with A-J-x. If that happens, South should duck on the way back.

In the above two examples a defender in West's position who held A-Q-9-x or A-K-9-x would normally win the first trick, so declarer need not fear a trap when he ducks in dummy on the second round. A new possibility is suggested by comparison of these two diagrams:

<pre>
        J 10 7 5 3   J 10 7 5 3
  Q 9 6 2   K 8   K Q 9 2   8 6
        A 4   A 4
</pre>

With the defending cards as shown on the left, the safety play we have been discussing,—low from dummy on the second round,—will save a trick. Thus, in diagram (2), West can trap an expert South by ducking on the second lead.

Establishing Side Suits

A form of play that is not exploited as much as it should be is the concession of an early trick when a side suit has to be established. The defender many not be able to judge the best play in the following situation:

<pre>
              J
  Q 8 7 4   K 9 2
              A 10 6 5 3
</pre>

This is a side suit from which tricks are needed, and declarer has not such a superfluity of trumps that he has any prospect of ruffing three times. He should begin by leading low from hand. If West goes in with the queen only one more round will be needed to establish three winners.

If you say that West should not put up the queen, then you can play on his nerves when the cards are as follows:

<pre>
              J
  Q 8 7 4   10 9 2
              A K 6 5 3
</pre>

Once again, if the trump position is not over-strong, South should begin by leading low towards the jack. West may duck, and if he does go in with the queen both players will tend to misplace the position of the remaining honors and this may well have a bearing on the subsequent defence.

It is also good play on many hands to begin with a low card when the long suit is on table.

A 8 6 4 3
Q

Better, in such situations, than leading the queen and hoping that West will not cover, is to lead a low card from the table. In so far as this is a deceptive play, it has a better chance of catching a strong than a weak defender, for a good player in East will by no means always put up the king. In addition, the play gains a trick by force of cards when either opponent has J-10-9 alone.

If the intermediate cards are strengthened the advantage of giving up the first trick is still greater.

Q

K 10 7 2   J 6
A 9 8 5 4 3

If nothing is known about the position of the king, the best way to start this side suit is by leading the queen from dummy, but if the king is likely to be held by West, low from South is the best opening maneuver. It is not unknown that West should duck; indeed, to go up with the king would be horrible play if partner had A-x or A-x-x. But say that West does go up with the king; on the next round the jack will fall to the ace and the best percentage play (see chapter 3) will be to run the 9 rather than ruff, playing East for J-10-x.

Making Use of the Pips

A good example of economy in the use of low cards is shown in the next deal:

Deal 116   ♠ A J 9 6 2   L - 6 ♡
                            ♡ K 4 3
                            ◇ A Q
                            ♣ 8 4 2

♠ 7 3   ♠ K Q 10 5 4
♡ 10 8   ♡ 7
◇ 9 8 7 4 3   ◇ K J 10 5
♣ J 10 7 6   ♣ K 9 5

                            ♠ 8
                            ♡ A Q J 9 6 5 2
                            ◇ 6 2
                            ♣ A Q 3

South played in 6 ♡ after East had opened the bidding with 1 ♠.

West led ♠ 7, and instead of going up automatically with the ace, declarer let this run. East won with 10 and returned a club. Winning with ♣ Q, South led ♡ A and overtook ♡ 9 with the king. Then he led ♠ J through East and, with two more entries to table, was able to establish a low spade for a discard from a minor suit .

The heart situation on the next hand has been the basis of many problem deals:

Deal 117

X - 6 ♠

```
              ♠ A 4 3
              ♡ A K 7 5 2
              ◇ K 6
              ♣ A Q 5
♠ J 5                         ♠ 10 2
♡ 9                           ♡ Q J 8 4 3
◇ Q J 10 8 4 3 2              ◇ 9 7 5
♣ J 9 7                       ♣ K 10 3
              ♠ K Q 9 8 7 6
              ♡ 10 6
              ◇ A
              ♣ 8 6 4 2
```

Playing in 6 ♠, South wins the diamond lead, draws two trumps with ♠ K-Q, and leads ♡ 6 to dummy's ♡ A. The contract is safe now if hearts split 4—2. South gives himself the chance of winning against 5—1 as well by cashing ◇ K and following with a low heart from table. East wins with the jack but any lead that he makes thereafter is to South's advantage.

```
              ♠ A
              ♡ K 7 5
              ◇ —
              ♣ A Q 5
♠ —                          ♠ —
♡ —                          ♡ Q 8 4
◇ J 10 8 4                   ◇ 9
♣ J 9 7                      ♣ K 10 3
              ♠ 9 8 7 6
              ♡ —
              ◇ —
              ♣ 8 6 4
```

Safety and Liaison

Many forms of suit establishment, from the simplest ducking play onwards, have the character of safety or liaison plays. Some examples of this kind follow.

```
              A K J 7 5 4 2
Q 10 9 8                      —
              6 3
```

To make sure of six tricks at notrump, with no side entry to table. South must duck from both hands on the first round. It is not safe to finesse the jack. One of the rarer brilliances in a deceptive way is for West to go in with the queen on the first round: that may weaken declarer's resolve and induce him to cover.

This is an extension of the same principle:

```
                    A K Q 10 6 4
    J 9 8 7 5                         —
                    3 2
```

To be sure of five tricks South must duck in both hands. The idea is fanciful but once again the play of the jack second hand may deflect South from his purpose.

This is a common situation at notrump:

```
                K Q 8 6 4 3
    10 5                         A J 9
                7 2
```

If South has only one other entry to dummy and can afford to lose two tricks, South must play low from both hands on the first round. If South goes up with an honor, East will kill the suit by ducking.

The same principle arises with K-Q-J-x-x opposite x-x and also in this position:

```
                A Q J 6 2
    9 4                         K 10 8 5
                7 3
```

Needing three tricks, with only one other entry to table, South must play low from dummy; if he finesses an honor, East will counter by holding off.

The next hand is a combined exercise in safety and liaison that belongs as much to the preceding chapter.

Deal **118**

```
                     ♠ 7 4                        H - 6 NT
                     ♡ A Q 10 7 5 3
                     ◇ K 5
                     ♣ 8 6 4
    ♠ J 9 5 3 2                          ♠ Q 10 8
    ♡ 8 4                                ♡ J 9 6 2
    ◇ 9                                  ◇ J 10 7 3
    ♣ J 10 9 5 2                         ♣ K 7
                     ♠ A K 6
                     ♡ K
                     ◇ A Q 8 6 4 2
                     ♣ A Q 3
```

Playing in 6 NT, South had the benefit of a club lead which appeared to give him twelve tricks so long as the diamonds were not 5—0. He cashed ♡ K, led a diamond to the king and discarded his two black losers on ♡ A-Q; but when he set out to clear diamonds he found the same player with the long diamond and the top heart and had to lose to both red jacks. The neat solution to this hand is that, after cashing ♡ K, South should play a low diamond from hand, ducking on the table; when both opponents follow, he has twelve tricks and is free from all entry trouble.

When a Side Suit is Blocked

When the run of a side suit is blocked because the top cards are isolated, one solution, as we saw in chapter 6 when studying the defence to such hands, is to play off the honors and allow an opponent to ruff. That would not be a good idea in a grand slam, however, and South had to find another solution on the next deal.

COFFEEHOUSE

The coffeehouse in old whist days
Was the site of tough whist frays,
Where slick players followed rules
Yet sharp tactics were their tools.

A shady trick today is termed
A coffeehouse. In deceit germed.
Modern bidding intonation
Gives illegal information.

A fast pass shows nothing pleases;
A slow pass means some good pieces.
A loud booming, ringing double
Says, "I have them trapped in trouble."

A come-on signal with snap of card
Warns the partner to be on guard.
Sometimes a good player will lapse
And stray in such coffeehouse traps.

Second hand with a singleton
For deceit plays hesitation;
Or from high card, a low slow toss,
The same swindle in double cross.

If you're fooled, it's just too bad:
It's you own fault thus "to be had."
Yet such practice doe not excuse
Perpetration of the low ruse.

If you revoked, can you resist
A second discard to persist
With aim to hide your first slip?
"They all do it," is the old quip.

To heckle is a nasty trick,
Those who do it are not my pick.
And too mean by a lot more
Is slight-of-hand with the score

A coffeehouse to help the luck
Marks one greedy for a fast buck.
If on must stoop so low to win,
It's a shame and mortal sin.

If in your game you spot a louse
Who often plays the coffeehouse,
My advice is the old refrain,
"Do not play with him again."

Deal 119
♠ A Q 8 5
♡ K 6
◇ 9
♣ Q 7 6 4 3 2

J - 7 ♠

♡ Q led

♠ K J 7 3 2
♡ A
◇ A 8 6 5 4
♣ A K

Playing in 7 ♠, South wins the first trick with ♡ A. He draws a round of trumps with ♠ K, to which both opponents follow. What next?

There is no problem if clubs are 3—2, so declarer must consider what to do if they are 4—1. He cannot draw three rounds of trumps before establishing the clubs for lack of entries to table. Can it help to cash one club, play a trump to dummy and discard ♣ K on the ♡ K? It seems doubtful, but try it out against this distribution:

♠ A Q 8 5
♡ K 6
◇ 9
♣ Q 7 6 4 3 2

♠ 4
♡ Q J 10 7 3
◇ Q 7 2
♣ J 10 9 8

♠ 10 9 6
♡ 9 8 5 4 2
◇ K J 10 3
♣ 5

♠ K J 7 3 2
♡ A
◇ A 8 6 5 4
♣ A K

The only play that succeeds is to take the discard on ♡ K, ruff a low club, play a third spade to dummy and ruff another club. Then the table is high.

It is a deceptive hand, for while the winning play readily presents itself, one has to play the cards over more than once to be assured of its effectiveness.

Chapter 15

THE VICE, THE WINKLE, AND THE STEPPING-STONE

(SQUEEZE STRIPS)

This chapter deals with the most important of the secondary squeeze positions. It is assumed that the commoner forms of squeeze play are familiar to any reader who has not dropped out by now. The Vice, the Winkle, and the Stepping-stone are names standing for different types of squeeze strips. These terms are introduced not for the sake of literary variation but because the use of descriptive titles may help to identify the different forms of play and assist the memory.

The secondary squeeze positions are those that do not conform to the usual pattern in which the declarer has a two-card menace and a one-card menace lying against the same opponent. Some other factor is present, an irregularity in the position of the menaces or in the entry position. At least twenty different types of squeeze can be constructed, but only a few of these are worth studying for purposes of practical play. The others are too rare, or too difficult, or of such a nature that a declarer going to and fro from the beginning of the play could avert such an artificial ending.

THE VICE (SQUEEZE SCOOP)

The vice describes the pressure upon a defender who holds two cards of equal rank that are needed to protect his partner's holding. The commonest example is Q-J protecting partner's ace.

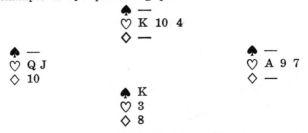

When South leads ♠ K, either at notrump or in a spade contract, the vice tightens on West's ♡ Q-J. The basic condition for such a squeeze is that in addition to the holding of ♡ K-10, spanning West's Q-J, either dummy or declarer must hold a second menace against West. Also, East must have no winning card apart from his control in the central suit.

If the second menace is in dummy it must be a two-card menace, for otherwise the defenders can ignore the threat. Here the diamond menace is transferred to North and there has to be an extra card:

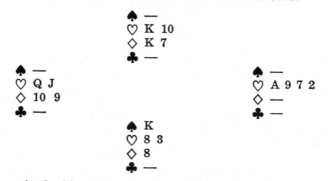

Once again the king of spades forces West to unguard a red suit. This hand gave rise to the ending:

Deal 120 ✳

```
                    ♠ J 6                           X - 4 ♠
                    ♡ K 10 5
                    ◇ K 7 6 3
                    ♣ J 8 4 2
    ♠ 8 5                                 ♠ 7 4 3
    ♡ Q J 6 4                             ♡ A 9 7 2
    ◇ 10 9 5 2                            ◇ J 4
    ♣ 6 5 3                               ♣ A K Q 10
                    ♠ A K Q 10 9 2
                    ♡ 8 3
                    ◇ A Q 8
                    ♣ 9 7
```

South played in 4 ♠ after East had opened at 1 ♣. West opened ♣ 6 and South ruffed the third round. After ♠ A and a spade to the jack, South ruffed the fourth club, a play that was necessary, as we shall see. Another round of trumps and two top diamonds produced the ending above:

On the last spade West threw ♡ J, whereupon ◇ 7 was thrown from dummy; a heart followed and East had to concede the last two tricks to the table.

It is clear that if South had not ruffed out East's fourth club, he could not have brought about this endplay. Also, he had to know what he was doing at the finish, for he would otherwise have played for a diamond break and been defeated. It is true that, in theory, the diamonds might have been breaking and West might have played ♡ J when not holding the queen; but fortunately not many people play as well as that.

Other holdings that lend themselves to this type of squeeze are 10-x opposite K-x when West holds Q-J and J-x opposite K-x when West holds the queen. Still more common is K-x-x opposite Q-9-x when an opponent holds J-10, as in the next deal.

In this ending the queen of diamonds has gone and when a heart is led East's ◇ J-10 is caught in a vice in the same way as West's ♡ Q-J in the previous example. Note that East has also to guard the two-card menace in spades. The full hand follows.

Deal 121

	♠ A K 3		X - 6 ♡
	♡ Q 10 8 6 4		
	◇ Q 7 2		
	♣ 10 6		

♠ J 10 9 7		♠ Q 6 5 2
♡ 7 5		♡ 2
◇ A 6 5 3		◇ J 10 8
♣ Q J 8		♣ 9 7 4 3 2

	♠ 8 4
	♡ A K J 9 3
	◇ K 9 4
	♣ A K 5

Playing in 6 ♡, South wins the spade lead in dummy, draws two trumps and leads a diamond to the queen. Three rounds of clubs follow, and more trumps, producing this ending:

	♠ A 3	
	♡ —	
	◇ 7 2	
	♣ —	

♠ 10 9		♠ Q 5
♡ —		♡ —
◇ A 6		◇ J 10
♣ —		♣ —

	♠ 8
	♡ J
	◇ K 9
	♣ —

On the lead of ♡ J West cannot bare his ◇ A, so he throws a spade; a diamond goes away from table and the vice closes on East's ◇ J-10.

For this contract to be made against any defence it was necessary that East hold ◇ J-10 and that West hold not more than three clubs. In practice, however, a player in West's position will often not appreciate the importance of keeping the side winner. If West had held four clubs, he would probably have come down to the same four cards.

The ending on the next hand is similar. No apology is made for that, for it is by playing over several hands of the same sort, and especially by trying to foresee the ending, that facility is acquired. Learning a new type of endplay is like mastering a tricky shot at golf or billiards. Once you find, in the course of practice, that you can play the shot several times in succession, you can put it away in your bag with confidence and look forward to opportunities for its execution.

Deal 122 ✳   X - 4 ♣

```
                   ♠ K 9 6 4
                   ♡ A K J
                   ◇ Q 3
                   ♣ A 10 6 5
   ♠ A 7 2                        ♠ J 10 3
   ♡ 9 6 5 4                      ♡ Q 10 8 3
   ◇ A K J                        ◇ 10 9 7 4 2
   ♣ J 9 2                        ♣ 3
                   ♠ Q 8 5
                   ♡ 7 2
                   ◇ 8 6 5
                   ♣ K Q 8 7 4
```

A part score for North-South led to this contentious auction:

South	West	North	East
—	1 NT	Double	2 ◇
3 ♣	3 ◇	4 ♣ (final bid)	

West led two top diamonds, followed by a heart, won on table. South came to hand with ♣ Q, ruffed his third diamond, and led three more rounds of trumps, leaving:

```
                   ♠ K 9 6
                   ♡ A J
                   ♣ —
   ♠ A 7 2                        ♠ J 10 3
   ♡ 9 6                          ♡ Q 10
   ♣ —                            ♣ —
                   ♠ Q 8 5
                   ♡ 7
                   ♣ 8
```

South placed West with ♠ A, but that was enough for his weak no-trump and the remaining honors, ♡ Q and ♠ J, could be attributed to East. If East held ♠ 10 as well, he could be crushed. South played his last club; West threw a heart and North a spade; East also had to throw a spade. Now South led a spade to the king, cashed ♡ A, and returned a spade, making the last trick with ♠ 8.

The heart menace is double if North's jack is instead a low heart.

THE WINKLE (SQUEEZE BLOCKED EXIT)

In the majority of squeeze strip positions a one-card menace that is controlled by both opponents is of no value against best defence. An exception occurs in the unbalanced guard squeeze,—that form of squeeze in which a defender has to keep a card to protect his partner from a finesse. In some of the secondary squeeze positions, however, when declarer can afford to lose one trick, a card that is third or fourth in rank can be promoted to first place. Study this ending:

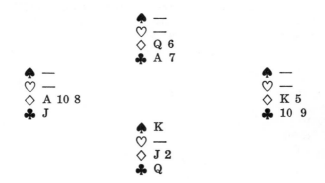

On the lead of ♠ K a diamond is thrown from dummy and East has no good discard. If East throws a low diamond, South cashes ♣ Q and follow with ◊ 2; if East attempts to unblock by throwing ◊ K, South will again cash ♣ Q and exit with ◊ 2, making the last trick with ◊ J.

The strange part about this ending is that South should be able to winkle a trick from the diamonds. That will happen only when there is a block such as exists in the club suit. Declarer has three top winners among the last four cards and it is only difficulty with entries that prevents him from cashing them. In the play of a full hand such difficulty can usually be overcome, which is why a squeeze of this sort is not familiar. Nevertheless, there are many hands on which there is no straightforward way of overcoming the entry problem.

Deal 123

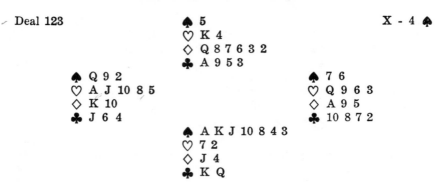

X - 4 ♠

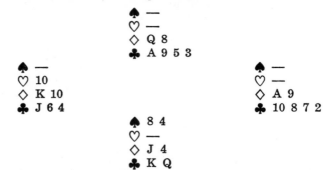

South played this hand in 4 ♠ and West opened ♡ A. The defenders can take four top tricks, but the play is not altogether clear and West played a second heart at trick 2. South finessed in spades and West played a third heart. Were it not for the entry situation, South would have ten tricks now. It is on such hands that the winkling process can be carried out. Three more rounds of trumps left these cards:

On the fifth trump West discarded a heart, North a diamond, and East a club. Then came ♣ K followed by the last trump. West threw a club and East a diamond, whereupon South cashed ♣ Q and exited with a diamond, making the last trick with ♣ A. East might have tried throwing ◇ A; then South would have made the last trick with ◇ J.

East-West could have saved the game by perfect defence: West must hold his last heart: then he can keep ◇ K and ♡ 10 for his last two cards and East can unblock in diamonds.

To make an extra trick in this way declarer does not require cards of such relatively august rank as the queen and jack. Even a 4 can exert a threat; that is what makes the winkle so charming and effective. With one or two changes in the diamond suit the ending might be:

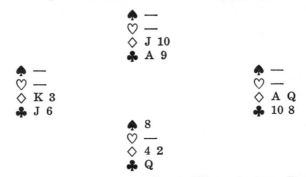

♠ —
♡ —
◇ J 10
♣ A 9

♠ —   ♠ —
♡ —   ♡ —
◇ K 3   ◇ A Q
♣ J 6   ♣ 10 8

♠ 8
♡ —
◇ 4 2
♣ Q

South leads ♠ 8, throwing a diamond from dummy. Best defence is for West to keep his clubs, but a defender will often go wrong and throw ♣ 6, judging that card to be of no value. After East's partner has let go a club, East's best chance is to throw ◇ A. Then South cashes ♣ Q and follows with ◇ 2. If West goes up with the king to save partner from being thrown in, South's ◇ 4 will win the last trick.

It comes to this, that whenever the run of a suit is obstructed by lack of entries there is an excellent chance of developing a surprise trick by means of a winkle. A reader who has studied the above few examples will have a new outlook on a hand such as the following:

Deal 124   ♠ 7 4 2   X - 2 NT
                            ♡ 9 7 5
                            ◇ K 10 6 5
                            ♣ 7 3 2

♠ 3 led
                            ♠ Q 10 6
                            ♡ Q 8 4
                            ◇ A Q
                            ♣ A K Q J 4

South opens 2 NT and all pass. The defenders take the first four tricks in spades but fail to find the heart switch, as can well happen when the honors are divided; instead, West exits with a club.

Most South players at this point would run five clubs, then lead ◇ A and overtake the queen, thinking that their only chance was to drop the jack. It would surprise them to be told that if West held ◇ J, the contract could not be defeated, while if East held that card, he might have

to perform a considerable feat of unblocking. Suppose, first, that West
has the diamond protection: then the end game is as shown below.

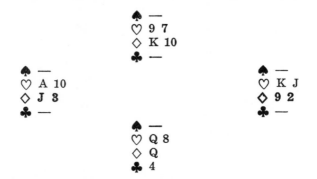

On the last club West heroically throws ♡ A. North discards a heart
and East a diamond. South now overtakes ◇ Q and leads a heart from
the table, winkling a trick for the queen.

Now transfer ◇ J and the ending may be:

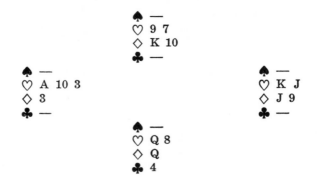

On the last club East may throw ♡ K, but the sacrifice is too late: if
he has A-J or K-J he must throw both honors to prevent a block in the
defence.

The Winkle against a Minor Tenace

There is one other occasion on which a trick can be winkled from an
unsupported queen or lower card. It is when a defender has a minor tenace and cannot allow himself to be thrown in.

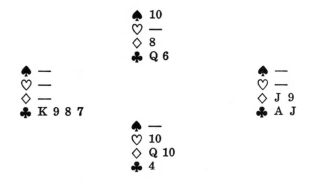

South, who has not been able to finesse the diamond when in dummy, leads ♡ 10. If East holds on to ♣ A he will be thrown in, and if East discards the ace, South will lead up to dummy's Q-6. This is the hand in which the ending arose:

Deal 125   ♠ Q J 10 7 4   X - 6 ♡
                               ♡ A J 6
                               ◇ 8 4 2
                               ♣ Q 6
      ♠ 8 2   ♠ K 9 5
      ♡ 8 7 4 3   ♡ —
      ◇ 3   ◇ K J 9 7 6 5
      ♣ K 9 8 7 3 2   ♣ A J 10 5
                               ♠ A 6 3
                               ♡ K Q 10 9 5 2
                               ◇ A Q 10
                               ♣ 4

South played in 6 ♡ after East had opened at 1 ◇. West opened ◇ 3 and South won with ace. Crossing to dummy on the second round of trumps, he ran ♠ Q followed by ♠ J. Then he ran off all the trumps and produced the ending shown above.

Declarer was unable to take the second finesse in diamonds on the last hand because West would ruff. At other times declarer is unable to take a marked finesse because he has no entry to the opposite hand or because the dummy has no card left of the finesse suit. This is a hand from the Masters Pairs some years ago on which I made twelve tricks without having much idea how it was done:

Deal 126   ♠ A 5   **X** - 3 NT
                            ♡ K 8 6 4 2
                            ◇ 10 5 3
                            ♣ K 7 4

    ♠ 7 6 4   ♠ Q 9 8 2
    ♡ 9 5   ♡ J 10 7 3
    ◇ K 8 4 2   ◇ A J 9 6
    ♣ 10 9 5 3   ♣ 8

                            ♠ K J 10 3
                            ♡ A Q
                            ◇ Q 7
                            ♣ A Q J 6 2

Sitting South, I opened 1 ♣ and over partner's response of 1 ♡ rebid 2 NT, a call that will not commend itself to modern scientific players. North raised to 3 NT and West, as expected, opened ♠ 7. East correctly withheld his queen and the jack won.

After cashing ♡ A-Q, I crossed to dummy with ♠ A and played ♡ K, discarding a diamond. After four rounds of clubs the position was:

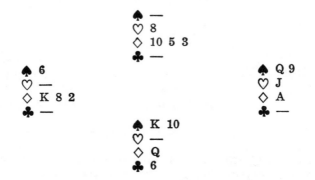

                            ♠ —
                            ♡ 8
                            ◇ 10 5 3
                            ♣ —

    ♠ 6   ♠ Q 9
    ♡ —   ♡ J
    ◇ K 8 2   ◇ A
    ♣ —   ♣ —

                            ♠ K 10
                            ♡ —
                            ◇ Q
                            ♣ 6

When the last club was led there was no defence to prevent South from taking three of the last four tricks. The most spectacular finish is for East to throw ◇ A, whereupon South cashes ♠ K and leads ◇ Q, winkling the last trick from dummy's ◇ 10.

THE STEPPING-STONE (SQUEEZE ENTRY)

The stepping-stone is a name for another type of squeeze strip in which declarer has sufficient tricks in top cards but cannot go conveniently from hand to hand. A blocked suit was present in most variations of the winkle squeeze, but the characteristic of those was that declarer succeeded in winkling an extra trick from a suit of which he held neither first nor second round control. In the stepping-stone the declarer exerts pressure in space to win the tricks that are rightfully his.

Like most forms of direct squeeze, the stepping-stone operates at two levels—when declarer has to make all the tricks and when he can afford to lose one trick. The second situation arises more often. Every player is familiar with an ending of this sort:

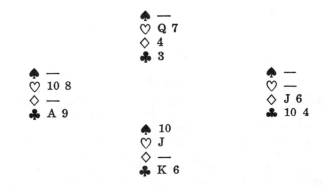

Playing in spades, South requires three of the last four tricks. In a sense he has them but he has not been able to cash ♡ J and make ♡ Q before drawing trumps. However, West is in difficulties on the last trump; when West throws ♣ 9 declarer cashes ♡ J and leads a club, using West's ace as a stepping-stone to the winning heart in dummy.

Note that this strip would not have been playable had South's heart not been of winning rank. South would have had the material for a squeeze, —two menaces against West,—but the timing would have been wrong.

CHEST YOUR CARDS

A peep is worth two finesses.
Eliminates all the guesses.

The snooper has such a long snout,
Grown from peeking in hands, no doubt.

Hold up your cards lest he can see
How to have a finessing spree.

He may smile and be chummy,
But he'll play it double dummy.

Or his smile may be a smirk
To hide his thought, "You're such a jerk!"

If you're playing for hard money,
It may not be very funny.

Take heed the adage least he reap,
For, "As ye show, so shall they peep."

All that is required for this sort of squeeze entry to work is that declarer should have an additional menace against the defender who controls the blocked position. If he had been aware of this simple requirement, declarer would have landed his slam on the next deal.

Deal 127

	♠ Q 10 8 4 2	X - 6 ♣
	♡ A Q 7 6	
	◇ K 10 6	
	♣ J	

♠ K 7 6 5		♠ J 9
♡ J 3		♡ 9 8 5 4 2
◇ J 8 5 4		◇ A Q 9 3
♣ 8 5 2		♣ 7 3

	♠ A 3	
	♡ K 10	
	◇ 7 2	
	♣ A K Q 10 9 6 4	

After North had opened the bidding rather light, South bid his way to 6 ♣. West thought he had to attack and made the unhappy choice of ♡ J. South won with the king and played several clubs. Then, judging from the discards that East held ◇ A, South tried to endplay East in diamonds and spades. After throwing a diamond from hand on the third round of hearts South came down to a three-card ending, keeping ♠ A-3 and ◇ 7, with ♠ Q-10 and ◇ K in dummy; then he exited with a diamond and went one down.

That East had length in hearts was obvious from the opening lead and if he could be placed with ◇ A as well, the defence would have no escape from the ending on the next page.

Limericks

UNINAMOUS

There was a young squirt named Boyd
Who liked to psyke on a void.
    When his psyke went beserk,
    Said partner, "You're a jerk!"
But opponents were both overjoyed.

ALMOST PERFECT

An arrogant player from Rhone
Would claim no error to atone.
    Partners he would blast.
    Now they duck fast
If they see him, around, alone.

Brijettes

MY PARTNER

My partner's a jolly good fellow,
Although often he sticks out his neck.
He pays no heed to what I bellow,
So we end up writing a check.

SOLUTION

What do you do with a Vienna Coup?
The problem is testing and real.

My one contribution to the final solution
Is to try hard to get a misdeal.
       John Thames, Birmingham, Alabama

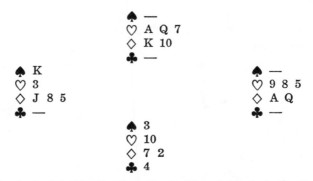

On the last club North discards ◇ 10 and East ◇ Q; South cashes ♡ 10 and exits with a diamond, using East as a stepping-stone to the last two hearts.

A Single Stride

Not quite so common, but still important, are those entry squeezes in which declarer can lose no further trick.

Playing in notrump, South has not been able to unblock hearts, but the ♠ 10 lead squeezes West in an unfamiliar way. He cannot throw a heart and if he lets go ♣ A South will cross to the other bank with a single stride and make the king.

If the heart length in this example were in the opposite hand, South having the queen and North the A-7, there would be an ordinary one-way squeeze. As it is, the two-card menace is in the same hand as the squeeze card; the compensating factor that makes the squeeze work is that North's ♡ Q is of winning rank. The squeeze is automatic, for it would work equally well against East if the East and West cards were interchanged.

One time to look for this squeeze is when declarer cannot unlock a side suit because of the danger of a ruff. The following hand was played in an international match:

Deal 128

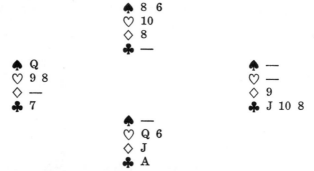

South was in 5 ◇ and the defence began with two top spades. South ruffed and crossed to dummy for a trump finesse. When West won with the king, he played a third spade, reducing South to two trumps. South crossed to dummy with a club, drew one diamond and laid down ♡ A-K; leaving:

After much thought declarer played ♣ A and led a low heart to the 10, playing for the hearts to break (the jack could have been a false card) or for the third trump to be with the long hearts.

If West had the last spade, as was likely from the play of that suit, there was not room for him to hold the last trump in addition to two hearts. All that South had to do was draw ◇ J and follow with ♣ A; West would have been caught in an entry squeeze of the stepping-stone variety.

The Jettison Squeeze

In the last two examples declarer's holding in the blocked suit has been A-7 opposite singleton queen and Q-6 opposite singleton 10. When the singleton is the topranking card, Q-x facing singleton ace, the only possibility is the rare and brilliant jettison squeeze.

Deal 129

Z - 3 NT

South played in 2 NT and West opened ♣ 10. South held up until the third round and played diamonds. West waited to see his partner's discard on the third diamond; then he switched to a heart, and the queen lost to East's ace. East cashed the thirteenth club, South threw a spade, and led ♠ 7, taken by the ace. After a fourth diamond the position was:

South led ◇ 10 and when West threw a heart, had only to keep his wits about him and discard ♡ K from dummy. This artistic squeeze can be played only against the left-hand opponent, that is, it is a one-way squeeze.

Reluctant Concession

A final example of the entry squeeze is from rubber bridge. It is one of my least happy memories. I suppose that almost every club player has someone in his circle against whom he plays with a special degree of contentiousness. For me, South, on the following deal was such an opponent: aggressive, slap-dash, achieving most of his effects by rough tactics against the weaker players.

Deal 130

	♠ K 9	Z - 4 ♣
	♡ A 10 6 4 2	
	◇ Q J 10	
	♣ A Q 8	

♠ 8 5 2		♠ A Q J 10 3
♡ J 8 7 3		♡ K Q 9
◇ 9 6 4 3		◇ A 5
♣ 10 5		♣ 7 4 2

	♠ 7 6 4	
	♡ 5	
	◇ K 8 7 2	
	♣ K J 9 6 3	

After a part-score battle South was declarer in 4 ♣, game. Sitting West, I led a spade to my partner's suit. After making two spade tricks East, playing a less than dynamic defence, led ace and another diamond. Declarer played ♣ Q and when the 10 fell, half showed his hand, suggesting nothing more to the play.

There was a pause during which East dwelt upon her outstanding trump. "Of course I ruff the spade and draw your trump," said South impatiently.

At this, my partner threw in her cards, as partners do. Such a concession is not binding on the other defender, however, and being experienced at doing battle with a jack and a 9 as my leading armaments, I had not yet lowered my flag. Ace of hearts and a heart ruff; spade ruff, another heart ruff; that would bring declarer down to one trump, and surely the diamonds would be blocked. Satisfied that this was so, I restored my partner's cards and asked South to play on. "Just as a matter of interest."

The play went as foreseen until the last trump was led as in the diagram on the next page.

Attempting to conceal my chagrin at this horrible turn of events, I threw in, conceding the last three tricks.

```
                    ♠ —
                    ♡ 10 6
                    ◇ Q
                    ♣ —
    ♠ —                              ♠ Q J
    ♡ J                              ♡ —
    ◇ 9 6                            ◇ —
    ♣ —                              ♣ 7
                    ♠ —
                    ♡ —
                    ◇ K 8
                    ♣ K
```

"I knew they were all mine," said South, passing the cards across for the next deal. "Cut, please."

Will Bridge Change?

By GEORGE S. COFFIN

Contract bridge was invented in 1925 by Harold S. Vanderbilt. It quickly spread in social sets. At first over 20 scoring schedules were used, of which two became popular and later were amalgamated. For 32 years the sport has been stabilized as the world's best card game.

A recent trend is the fantastic growth of duplicate. The American Contract Bridge League (ACBL) had 8,000 members 12 years ago,—today has nearly 100,000. Duplicate games make good party bridge for weak players and a skill contest without stakes for all players.

Odd Types of Bridge

During the past five decades scores of odd types of bridge have come and gone. Of these only two-handed and three-handed bridge have stood the test of time for utilitarian reasons. We had *Nullos* to lose tricks at notrump, *Reversi*, Ellicott's game with the joker, goulashes, contract whist, and five-suit bridge. Also the interesting elective partnership principle was introduced in 1912 and it reappeared twice in 1936 and 1937. Here a player elected his partner with his bid. If dissatisfied, the electee could break the bond if he elected a different partner and bid higher. Details of these and other games are on pages 121-125 of our *Learn Bridge The Easy Way*, Branford, 1950. This book concluded, "Gadgets and novelties in bridge are fun occasionally, but for a steady diet, you are advised to concentrate on improving your regular game for lasting enjoyment."

The Swing To Point Count

The grand shift from honor tricks to the 4-3-2-1 point count during the past decade reflects popular trend. Bridge players found point count easier and more accurate to use.

Originally point count was used only to value high cards at notrump, and the first record that we know appears on page

26 of *Auction Tactics* by Bryant McCampbell, Dodd Mead, 1915.

According to page 64 of *Learn Bridge The Easy Way*, the 4-3-2-1 count "originated in Italy with playing cards circa 1260 A.D." It was used to score high cards won on tricks then (and still today) in the game of *I Tarocchi*, the "great root ancestor of all games of the whist family."

Shape points (for long and short suits) are a recent innovation,—in popular use barely a decade. On 23 October 1958 the *New York Sunday Times* credited Fred L. Karpin with being the first to popularize the 4-3-2-1 point count including shape points. Later Charles H. Goren wrote *Point Count Bidding*. He assigned no value for suit length in opening bids but did so indirectly by counting 3 points for a void suit, 2 for a singleton and 1 for a doubleton. Responder with four supporting trumps for ruffing counted 5 points for a void, 3 for a singleton and 1 for a doubleton. These exact scales were first published on page 40 of our quaint little out-of-print book, *Winning Duplicate*, Bruce Humphries, 1933.

The Italian Influence

The recent three successive Italian world victories have painfully raised two vital questions. Do American's losses stem from systemic inferiority? Or from poor bridge?

Wrote Edgar Kaplan in the June 1959 *Bridge World*. "In the 1959 match the Italian superiority in slam bidding accounted for nearly the entire 50 IMP margin of victory." Later he mentioned that Americans used only two slam tools, Blackwood and cue bids, whereas the Italians employed their entire kit of some dozen well-honed slam bid instruments.

Albert H. Morehead in the *Sunday Times* and others fingered poor bridge playing for our losses. Mr. Goren has repeatedly stated in public, "There is nothing wrong with American bridge," implying a smiliar view.

Italian quartet captain Albert H. Perroux in the March 1959 *Bridge World* fingered both factors, taking a more realistic view. He wrote, "The American systems, like all natural systems, are adapted for the millions who play rubber bridge; the artificial (Italian) systems, full of conventions, difficult to memorize, even more difficult to apply, provide an immense advantage in competitive bridge at the highest level."

Sr. Perroux likened American methods to the good old family automobile designed for comfort and safety, and Italian methods to a sleek racer designed for acceleration and breakneck speed.

Sr. Perroux also stated, " . . . the Americans have some excellent players, the best in the world, but I have not yet seen them compose a TEAM."

All this has stimulated the sale of recent books on Italian methods despite the current ban on Italian systems in ACBL and English Bridge Union tournaments.

The New Revolt in Bridge

All this has created unrest. The bridge public suspects something wrong with standard bidding as promoted by Goren. All this has stimulated the idea men of bridge. They are offering changes, some rather drastic ones.

Rex Bridge is one, invented by Sten Lundberg of Sweden. Special premiums are awarded for contracts of 4 NT, 5 ♡ and 5 ♠, a good idea. A new bid is introduced, Rex, a special notrump contract with the rank of all cards changed to king top (hence the name, Rex), queen second, and so on down to ace bottom. Rex overcalls any suit but bows to any regular notrump call. Rex Bridge is strictly a passing novelty.

The Forest of Weeds

Pity the poor average player! How can he hope to cope with literally scores of conventions, Italian and otherwise? Norman Squire in *A Guide to Bridge Conventions,* Duckworth, 1958, describes 120 basic conventions plus scores of variations. ACBL directors are fighting a losing war against the influx of conventions. Often barred are such specific items as the Woodson Two-Way Notrump and Jacoby Transfer Bids. This practice, albeit commendable to protect the field, is like hacking the tops off weeds. Inventive genius simply sprouts new and strange systemic gadgets to replace those barred.

The Four-Card Rule

We suggested the four-card rule in the May 1959 *South African Bridge* to kill all the weeds in one fell swoop.

In each deal, no player may bid a suit of less than four cards for the first time in the auction below the level of four. A suggested penalty for offence, if discovered before the score is entered, is 200 points.

The four-card rule would not bar cue bids in slam calling, nor at any level in an enemy-bid suit. But this rule would bar artificial openings.

In the October 1958 *British Bridge World* Terence Reese wrote, "I advocate: The use of suit bids as ciphers, bearing no relation to the suit named, to be barred with two exceptions, 2 ♣ (opening) and 2 ◇ (negative response). Fishbein, Stayman, Texas, Neopolitan, Jacoby Transfer, — the game can well get along without any of them. In fact, more people would want to play it."

Bridge Magazine editor Ewart Kempson, in his letter to us dated 22 June 1959, wrote, "I said all this (about artificial conventions in general) in 1933, which is more than a quarter of a century ago."

Adverse Use

Let us review a trend of the past. Does an artificial bid or cue bid showing the exact suit and rank of a card expose that card legally?

Mr. Kempson's letter continued, "In the 1932 international code, agreed by the New York Whist Club, an exposed card during the auction was any card held by a player if he said anything indicating that he holds it. In the 4-5 NT Convention (Culbertson) it was possible for players to name to each other five cards (aces and trump king) during the auction. Yet the Whist Club ignored the ruling given both by the Portland (Club) and Commission Francais . . . In 1934 the Portland Club named the 4-5 NT illegal . . . "

During the following years the ruling became obsolete by adverse use and it was dropped from the Laws of Bridge.

Clearly the principle of the four-card rule is favored today. With the idea that a four-card rule may be adopted, we devised a convention called Natural over Notrump detailed in the January and February 1959 *Bridge Magazine*. The convention is simple. A 2 ♣ or 2 ◊ takeout of 1 NT guarantees four cards of the suit bid, is forcing once, and it asks opener to bid a four-card major. A major suit takeout of notrump remains unchanged as a signoff.

A mathematical analysis revealed the astounding fact that Natural over Notrump is effective 49 times out of 50 when Stayman could be used instead. And a special bid was offered to cover that rare 50th time. Also, a great advantage is fast discovery of a 4-4 minor-suit fit for a slam, something Stayman users often miss.

New Bridge Mathematics

The above was substantiated by correlating two types of tables of frequency. Hand pattern frequencies have been known for years, but frequencies of high-card point count were unknown. The latter are the missing links of system design, which for years has been based on painfully slow trial-by-error. At my request, Colonel Roy L. Telfer of England computed by two weeks' hard labor Telfer's Table, percentage frequencies of being dealt the various amounts of high-card points, from 0 to 37. A very simplified form of this table is on page 50 of our new *Bridge on Deck*. A justified criticism by Col. Telfer of our

articles based on the *a priori* assumption of holdings before the auction was our application of his table to holdings of responder *after* his partner had opened 1 NT. In this case, secondary tables are necessary to compensate for the *a priori* knowledge of 16 to 18 points held by opener if using the strong notrump. While not mentioned in our articles, interpolations were made.

Bridge authorities sorely need a full set of point-count frequency tables, one each for expectancies of responder to an opening suit bid of one, two, three, when partner has been doubled, or overcalled, etc. The task of computing such tables is colossal, requiring electronic computers. Until this job is done, no one can hope to find or know the best mathematical bid for every position in the auction.

Nascent Suit Bridge

Another idea, proposed on page 295 of *Bridge Quarterly*, is nascent suits.

In each deal suits have no rank before the auction. The first suit called becomes the higher-ranking major; the second suit called, which must be at a higher level, becomes the second major; and the third suit called the higher-ranking minor.

This eliminates one-over-one because a player must go one level higher to bid a new suit. But the first suit called outranks all others in the later auction. No player will want to open a short suit artificially or as a psychic and deprive his side of the chance to establish a good suit as a major.

Equal Suit Bridge

A similar idea in reverse has just been introduced by Rawley D. Haas of Gaffney, South Carolina. All four suits may be called in any order at the same level. Stated another way, any *unbid* suit will overbid any suit bid previously; but to bid over notrump, or to bid a suit previously bid at a specific level, a player must bid it in a higher level. For example, note this auction:

South	West	North	East
1 ♠	1 ♡	1 ◇	1 ♣
1 NT	2 ♡	2 ◇	etc.

The flaw in equal suits is that a short-suit or transfer-bid system offers great advantages. Opener bids one of his *shortest* suit, hears partner respond, then bids his real suit still in the one-level! Or opener can bid the suit one step under his real suit (by conventional suit ranks) and partner with less than 6 points can transfer to opener's real suit as a signoff. To prevent all this, the four-card rule is essential.

New Ways to Score

Mr. Haas' second big feature is the geometric progression of premiums for every successful contract of two and up, beginning at 50 points. The premium for a three-bid is 100 points, for a four-bid 200, and so on up to 1600 for a grand slam. Vulnerability, game premiums, and major and minor suits are eliminated. Trump contracts score 20 points per trick, notrump 40. The present vulnerable scale of penalties is used. This idea deserves study.

Another idea needing study is two-way scoring. In this, the defenders themselves score a partial, game, or slam if they defeat such a contract sufficiently. It works thus: If declarer goes down one, neither side scores; if down two, defenders score one-half (toward game at rubber bridge) of what declarer would make if successful; if down three, amount of declarer's contract, if down more, 50 points per setting trick exceeding three are added. A double would elevate defenders' award one grade, a redouble two grades, with surplus defeat tricks worth 100 and 200 each respectively.

Suppose 4 ♠ doubled goes down three. Opponents score game (for the two-down level) plus 100 points.

Lawmakers Take Notice!

Tobias Stone in the July 1959 *Bridge World* offered new IMP with half points

to eliminate inequities. The idea is good, but why the detour? The IMP scale at best is a makeshift proposition. The simple *direct* way is to modify total points for knockout team-of-four play. Eliminate vulnerability and reduce game and slam premiums to obtain the same result to prevent excessive swings. Such an improved scoring schedule could do away with match pointing of pair games,—a boon to harassed tournament directors.

A new unpublished idea is target bridge. In this declarer must fulfill his contract on the nose without any overtrick. For example, if he wins 12 tricks at 4 ♡, he scores exactly as if he went down two! This would create plenty of action in the play!

In concluding we recommend that the ACBL spend some of its huge surplus fund for research on the rub-of-the-green by four (or more) bridge experts to test all new games and ideas. Every big corporation spends millions annually for research. How much is spent on bridge?

We dare not predict what new form bridge will assume, if any. Two detrimental features that should and can be corrected are: (1) too many conventions and (2) abortive scoring at duplicate. Players yearn, subconsciously at least, for something new and simplified, yet exciting.

LITERATURE CITED

Auction Tactics by Bryant McCampbell
Bridge on Deck by Coffin
Equal Suit Bridge by Rawley D. Haas
Guide to Bridge Conventions by Squire
Learn Bridge the Easy Way by Coffin
Point Count Bidding by Goren
Winning Duplicate by Coffin
Bridge Magazine, Leeds, England
Bridge Quarterly, Chestnut Hill
Bridge World, New York
British Bridge World, London
South African Bridge, Johannesburg
New York Sunday Times

A CATALOG OF SELECTED
DOVER BOOKS
IN ALL FIELDS OF INTEREST

A CATALOG OF SELECTED DOVER
BOOKS IN ALL FIELDS OF INTEREST

CONCERNING THE SPIRITUAL IN ART, Wassily Kandinsky. Pioneering work by father of abstract art. Thoughts on color theory, nature of art. Analysis of earlier masters. 12 illustrations. 80pp. of text. 5⅜ × 8½.   23411-8 Pa. $3.95

ANIMALS: 1,419 Copyright-Free Illustrations of Mammals, Birds, Fish, Insects, etc., Jim Harter (ed.). Clear wood engravings present, in extremely lifelike poses, over 1,000 species of animals. One of the most extensive pictorial sourcebooks of its kind. Captions. Index. 284pp. 9 × 12.   23766-4 Pa. $12.95

CELTIC ART: The Methods of Construction, George Bain. Simple geometric techniques for making Celtic interlacements, spirals, Kells-type initials, animals, humans, etc. Over 500 illustrations. 160pp. 9 × 12. (USO)   22923-8 Pa. $9.95

AN ATLAS OF ANATOMY FOR ARTISTS, Fritz Schider. Most thorough reference work on art anatomy in the world. Hundreds of illustrations, including selections from works by Vesalius, Leonardo, Goya, Ingres, Michelangelo, others. 593 illustrations. 192pp. 7⅛ × 10¼.   20241-0 Pa. $9.95

CELTIC HAND STROKE-BY-STROKE (Irish Half-Uncial from "The Book of Kells"): An Arthur Baker Calligraphy Manual, Arthur Baker. Complete guide to creating each letter of the alphabet in distinctive Celtic manner. Covers hand position, strokes, pens, inks, paper, more. Illustrated. 48pp. 8¼ × 11.
                    24336-2 Pa. $3.95

EASY ORIGAMI, John Montroll. Charming collection of 32 projects (hat, cup, pelican, piano, swan, many more) specially designed for the novice origami hobbyist. Clearly illustrated easy-to-follow instructions insure that even beginning papercrafters will achieve successful results. 48pp. 8¼ × 11.   27298-2 Pa. $2.95

THE COMPLETE BOOK OF BIRDHOUSE CONSTRUCTION FOR WOOD-WORKERS, Scott D. Campbell. Detailed instructions, illustrations, tables. Also data on bird habitat and instinct patterns. Bibliography. 3 tables. 63 illustrations in 15 figures. 48pp. 5¼ × 8½.   24407-5 Pa. $1.95

BLOOMINGDALE'S ILLUSTRATED 1886 CATALOG: Fashions, Dry Goods and Housewares, Bloomingdale Brothers. Famed merchants' extremely rare catalog depicting about 1,700 products: clothing, housewares, firearms, dry goods, jewelry, more. Invaluable for dating, identifying vintage items. Also, copyright-free graphics for artists, designers. Co-published with Henry Ford Museum & Greenfield Village. 160pp. 8¼ × 11.   25780-0 Pa. $9.95

HISTORIC COSTUME IN PICTURES, Braun & Schneider. Over 1,450 costumed figures in clearly detailed engravings—from dawn of civilization to end of 19th century. Captions. Many folk costumes. 256pp. 8⅜ × 11¾.   23150-X Pa. $11.95

STICKLEY CRAFTSMAN FURNITURE CATALOGS, Gustav Stickley and L. & J. G. Stickley. Beautiful, functional furniture in two authentic catalogs from 1910. 594 illustrations, including 277 photos, show settles, rockers, armchairs, reclining chairs, bookcases, desks, tables. 183pp. 6½ × 9¼. 23838-5 Pa. $9.95

AMERICAN LOCOMOTIVES IN HISTORIC PHOTOGRAPHS: 1858 to 1949, Ron Ziel (ed.). A rare collection of 126 meticulously detailed official photographs, called "builder portraits," of American locomotives that majestically chronicle the rise of steam locomotive power in America. Introduction. Detailed captions. xi + 129pp. 9 × 12. 27393-8 Pa. $12.95

AMERICA'S LIGHTHOUSES: An Illustrated History, Francis Ross Holland, Jr. Delightfully written, profusely illustrated fact-filled survey of over 200 American lighthouses since 1716. History, anecdotes, technological advances, more. 240pp. 8 × 10¾. 25576-X Pa. $11.95

TOWARDS A NEW ARCHITECTURE, Le Corbusier. Pioneering manifesto by founder of "International School." Technical and aesthetic theories, views of industry, economics, relation of form to function, "mass-production split" and much more. Profusely illustrated. 320pp. 6⅛ × 9¼. (USO) 25023-7 Pa. $9.95

HOW THE OTHER HALF LIVES, Jacob Riis. Famous journalistic record, exposing poverty and degradation of New York slums around 1900, by major social reformer. 100 striking and influential photographs. 233pp. 10 × 7⅞.
22012-5 Pa $10.95

FRUIT KEY AND TWIG KEY TO TREES AND SHRUBS, William M. Harlow. One of the handiest and most widely used identification aids. Fruit key covers 120 deciduous and evergreen species; twig key 160 deciduous species. Easily used. Over 300 photographs. 126pp. 5⅜ × 8½. 20511-8 Pa. $3.95

COMMON BIRD SONGS, Dr. Donald J. Borror. Songs of 60 most common U.S. birds: robins, sparrows, cardinals, bluejays, finches, more—arranged in order of increasing complexity. Up to 9 variations of songs of each species.
Cassette and manual 99911-4 $8.95

ORCHIDS AS HOUSE PLANTS, Rebecca Tyson Northen. Grow cattleyas and many other kinds of orchids—in a window, in a case, or under artificial light. 63 illustrations. 148pp. 5⅜ × 8½. 23261-1 Pa. $4.95

MONSTER MAZES, Dave Phillips. Masterful mazes at four levels of difficulty. Avoid deadly perils and evil creatures to find magical treasures. Solutions for all 32 exciting illustrated puzzles. 48pp. 8¼ × 11. 26005-4 Pa. $2.95

MOZART'S DON GIOVANNI (DOVER OPERA LIBRETTO SERIES), Wolfgang Amadeus Mozart. Introduced and translated by Ellen H. Bleiler. Standard Italian libretto, with complete English translation. Convenient and thoroughly portable—an ideal companion for reading along with a recording or the performance itself. Introduction. List of characters. Plot summary. 121pp. 5¼ × 8½.
24944-1 Pa. $2.95

TECHNICAL MANUAL AND DICTIONARY OF CLASSICAL BALLET, Gail Grant. Defines, explains, comments on steps, movements, poses and concepts. 15-page pictorial section. Basic book for student, viewer. 127pp. 5⅜ × 8½.
21843-0 Pa. $4.95

BRASS INSTRUMENTS: Their History and Development, Anthony Baines. Authoritative, updated survey of the evolution of trumpets, trombones, bugles, cornets, French horns, tubas and other brass wind instruments. Over 140 illustrations and 48 music examples. Corrected and updated by author. New preface. Bibliography. 320pp. 5⅜ × 8½. 27574-4 Pa. $9.95

HOLLYWOOD GLAMOR PORTRAITS, John Kobal (ed.). 145 photos from 1926–49. Harlow, Gable, Bogart, Bacall; 94 stars in all. Full background on photographers, technical aspects. 160pp. 8⅜ × 11¼. 23352-9 Pa. $11.95

MAX AND MORITZ, Wilhelm Busch. Great humor classic in both German and English. Also 10 other works: "Cat and Mouse," "Plisch and Plumm," etc. 216pp. 5⅜ × 8½. 20181-3 Pa. $5.95

THE RAVEN AND OTHER FAVORITE POEMS, Edgar Allan Poe. Over 40 of the author's most memorable poems: "The Bells," "Ulalume," "Israfel," "To Helen," "The Conqueror Worm," "Eldorado," "Annabel Lee," many more. Alphabetic lists of titles and first lines. 64pp. 5³⁄₁₆ × 8¼. 26685-0 Pa. $1.00

SEVEN SCIENCE FICTION NOVELS, H. G. Wells. The standard collection of the great novels. Complete, unabridged. First Men in the Moon, Island of Dr. Moreau, War of the Worlds, Food of the Gods, Invisible Man, Time Machine, In the Days of the Comet. Total of 1,015pp. 5⅜ × 8½. (USO) 20264-X Clothbd. $29.95

AMULETS AND SUPERSTITIONS, E. A. Wallis Budge. Comprehensive discourse on origin, powers of amulets in many ancient cultures: Arab, Persian, Babylonian, Assyrian, Egyptian, Gnostic, Hebrew, Phoenician, Syriac, etc. Covers cross, swastika, crucifix, seals, rings, stones, etc. 584pp. 5⅜ × 8½. 23573-4 Pa. $12.95

RUSSIAN STORIES/PYCCKNE PACCKA3bl: A Dual-Language Book, edited by Gleb Struve. Twelve tales by such masters as Chekhov, Tolstoy, Dostoevsky, Pushkin, others. Excellent word-for-word English translations on facing pages, plus teaching and study aids, Russian/English vocabulary, biographical/critical introductions, more. 416pp. 5⅜ × 8½. 26244-8 Pa. $8.95

PHILADELPHIA THEN AND NOW: 60 Sites Photographed in the Past and Present, Kenneth Finkel and Susan Oyama. Rare photographs of City Hall, Logan Square, Independence Hall, Betsy Ross House, other landmarks juxtaposed with contemporary views. Captures changing face of historic city. Introduction. Captions. 128pp. 8¼ × 11. 25790-8 Pa. $9.95

AIA ARCHITECTURAL GUIDE TO NASSAU AND SUFFOLK COUNTIES, LONG ISLAND, The American Institute of Architects, Long Island Chapter, and the Society for the Preservation of Long Island Antiquities. Comprehensive, well-researched and generously illustrated volume brings to life over three centuries of Long Island's great architectural heritage. More than 240 photographs with authoritative, extensively detailed captions. 176pp. 8¼ × 11. 26946-9 Pa. $14.95

NORTH AMERICAN INDIAN LIFE: Customs and Traditions of 23 Tribes, Elsie Clews Parsons (ed.). 27 fictionalized essays by noted anthropologists examine religion, customs, government, additional facets of life among the Winnebago, Crow, Zuni, Eskimo, other tribes. 480pp. 6⅛ × 9¼. 27377-6 Pa. $10.95

CATALOG OF DOVER BOOKS

FRANK LLOYD WRIGHT'S HOLLYHOCK HOUSE, Donald Hoffmann. Lavishly illustrated, carefully documented study of one of Wright's most controversial residential designs. Over 120 photographs, floor plans, elevations, etc. Detailed perceptive text by noted Wright scholar. Index. 128pp. 9¼ × 10¾.
27133-1 Pa. $11.95

THE MALE AND FEMALE FIGURE IN MOTION: 60 Classic Photographic Sequences, Eadweard Muybridge. 60 true-action photographs of men and women walking, running, climbing, bending, turning, etc., reproduced from rare 19th-century masterpiece. vi + 121pp. 9 × 12.
24745-7 Pa. $10.95

1001 QUESTIONS ANSWERED ABOUT THE SEASHORE, N. J. Berrill and Jacquelyn Berrill. Queries answered about dolphins, sea snails, sponges, starfish, fishes, shore birds, many others. Covers appearance, breeding, growth, feeding, much more. 305pp. 5¼ × 8¼.
23366-9 Pa. $7.95

GUIDE TO OWL WATCHING IN NORTH AMERICA, Donald S. Heintzelman. Superb guide offers complete data and descriptions of 19 species: barn owl, screech owl, snowy owl, many more. Expert coverage of owl-watching equipment, conservation, migrations and invasions, etc. Guide to observing sites. 84 illustrations. xiii + 193pp. 5⅜ × 8½.
27344-X Pa. $8.95

MEDICINAL AND OTHER USES OF NORTH AMERICAN PLANTS: A Historical Survey with Special Reference to the Eastern Indian Tribes, Charlotte Erichsen-Brown. Chronological historical citations document 500 years of usage of plants, trees, shrubs native to eastern Canada, northeastern U.S. Also complete identifying information. 343 illustrations. 544pp. 6½ × 9¼.
25951-X Pa. $12.95

STORYBOOK MAZES, Dave Phillips. 23 stories and mazes on two-page spreads: Wizard of Oz, Treasure Island, Robin Hood, etc. Solutions. 64pp. 8¼ × 11.
23628-5 Pa. $2.95

NEGRO FOLK MUSIC, U.S.A., Harold Courlander. Noted folklorist's scholarly yet readable analysis of rich and varied musical tradition. Includes authentic versions of over 40 folk songs. Valuable bibliography and discography. xi + 324pp. 5⅜ × 8½.
27350-4 Pa. $7.95

MOVIE-STAR PORTRAITS OF THE FORTIES, John Kobal (ed.). 163 glamor, studio photos of 106 stars of the 1940s: Rita Hayworth, Ava Gardner, Marlon Brando, Clark Gable, many more. 176pp. 8⅜ × 11¼.
23546-7 Pa. $11.95

BENCHLEY LOST AND FOUND, Robert Benchley. Finest humor from early 30s, about pet peeves, child psychologists, post office and others. Mostly unavailable elsewhere. 73 illustrations by Peter Arno and others. 183pp. 5⅜ × 8½.
22410-4 Pa. $5.95

YEKL and THE IMPORTED BRIDEGROOM AND OTHER STORIES OF YIDDISH NEW YORK, Abraham Cahan. Film Hester Street based on Yekl (1896). Novel, other stories among first about Jewish immigrants on N.Y.'s East Side. 240pp. 5⅜ × 8½.
22427-9 Pa. $6.95

SELECTED POEMS, Walt Whitman. Generous sampling from *Leaves of Grass*. Twenty-four poems include "I Hear America Singing," "Song of the Open Road," "I Sing the Body Electric," "When Lilacs Last in the Dooryard Bloom'd," "O Captain! My Captain!"—all reprinted from an authoritative edition. Lists of titles and first lines. 128pp. 5³⁄₁₆ × 8¼.
26878-0 Pa. $1.00

THE BEST TALES OF HOFFMANN, E. T. A. Hoffmann. 10 of Hoffmann's most important stories: "Nutcracker and the King of Mice," "The Golden Flowerpot," etc. 458pp. 5⅜ × 8½. 21793-0 Pa. $8.95

FROM FETISH TO GOD IN ANCIENT EGYPT, E. A. Wallis Budge. Rich detailed survey of Egyptian conception of "God" and gods, magic, cult of animals, Osiris, more. Also, superb English translations of hymns and legends. 240 illustrations. 545pp. 5⅜ × 8½. 25803-3 Pa. $11.95

FRENCH STORIES/CONTES FRANÇAIS: A Dual-Language Book, Wallace Fowlie. Ten stories by French masters, Voltaire to Camus: "Micromegas" by Voltaire; "The Atheist's Mass" by Balzac; "Minuet" by de Maupassant; "The Guest" by Camus, six more. Excellent English translations on facing pages. Also French-English vocabulary list, exercises, more. 352pp. 5⅜ × 8½. 26443-2 Pa. $8.95

CHICAGO AT THE TURN OF THE CENTURY IN PHOTOGRAPHS: 122 Historic Views from the Collections of the Chicago Historical Society, Larry A. Viskochil. Rare large-format prints offer detailed views of City Hall, State Street, the Loop, Hull House, Union Station, many other landmarks, circa 1904–1913. Introduction. Captions. Maps. 144pp. 9⅜ × 12¼. 24656-6 Pa. $12.95

OLD BROOKLYN IN EARLY PHOTOGRAPHS, 1865–1929, William Lee Younger. Luna Park, Gravesend race track, construction of Grand Army Plaza, moving of Hotel Brighton, etc. 157 previously unpublished photographs. 165pp. 8⅞ × 11¾. 23587-4 Pa. $13.95

THE MYTHS OF THE NORTH AMERICAN INDIANS, Lewis Spence. Rich anthology of the myths and legends of the Algonquins, Iroquois, Pawnees and Sioux, prefaced by an extensive historical and ethnological commentary. 36 illustrations. 480pp. 5⅜ × 8½. 25967-6 Pa. $8.95

AN ENCYCLOPEDIA OF BATTLES: Accounts of Over 1,560 Battles from 1479 B.C. to the Present, David Eggenberger. Essential details of every major battle in recorded history from the first battle of Megiddo in 1479 B.C. to Grenada in 1984. List of Battle Maps. New Appendix covering the years 1967–1984. Index. 99 illustrations. 544pp. 6½ × 9¼. 24913-1 Pa. $14.95

SAILING ALONE AROUND THE WORLD, Captain Joshua Slocum. First man to sail around the world, alone, in small boat. One of great feats of seamanship told in delightful manner. 67 illustrations. 294pp. 5⅜ × 8½. 20326-3 Pa. $5.95

ANARCHISM AND OTHER ESSAYS, Emma Goldman. Powerful, penetrating, prophetic essays on direct action, role of minorities, prison reform, puritan hypocrisy, violence, etc. 271pp. 5⅜ × 8½. 22484-8 Pa. $5.95

MYTHS OF THE HINDUS AND BUDDHISTS, Ananda K. Coomaraswamy and Sister Nivedita. Great stories of the epics; deeds of Krishna, Shiva, taken from puranas, Vedas, folk tales; etc. 32 illustrations. 400pp. 5⅜ × 8½. 21759-0 Pa. $9.95

BEYOND PSYCHOLOGY, Otto Rank. Fear of death, desire of immortality, nature of sexuality, social organization, creativity, according to Rankian system. 291pp. 5⅜ × 8½. 20485-5 Pa. $8.95

A THEOLOGICO-POLITICAL TREATISE, Benedict Spinoza. Also contains unfinished Political Treatise. Great classic on religious liberty, theory of government on common consent. R. Elwes translation. Total of 421pp. 5⅜ × 8½. 20249-6 Pa. $8.95

MY BONDAGE AND MY FREEDOM, Frederick Douglass. Born a slave, Douglass became outspoken force in antislavery movement. The best of Douglass' autobiographies. Graphic description of slave life. 464pp. 5⅜ × 8½.　22457-0 Pa. $8.95

FOLLOWING THE EQUATOR: A Journey Around the World, Mark Twain. Fascinating humorous account of 1897 voyage to Hawaii, Australia, India, New Zealand, etc. Ironic, bemused reports on peoples, customs, climate, flora and fauna, politics, much more. 197 illustrations. 720pp. 5⅜ × 8½.　26113-1 Pa. $15.95

THE PEOPLE CALLED SHAKERS, Edward D. Andrews. Definitive study of Shakers: origins, beliefs, practices, dances, social organization, furniture and crafts, etc. 33 illustrations. 351pp. 5⅜ × 8½.　21081-2 Pa. $8.95

THE MYTHS OF GREECE AND ROME, H. A. Guerber. A classic of mythology, generously illustrated, long prized for its simple, graphic, accurate retelling of the principal myths of Greece and Rome, and for its commentary on their origins and significance. With 64 illustrations by Michelangelo, Raphael, Titian, Rubens, Canova, Bernini and others. 480pp. 5⅜ × 8½.　27584-1 Pa. $9.95

PSYCHOLOGY OF MUSIC, Carl E. Seashore. Classic work discusses music as a medium from psychological viewpoint. Clear treatment of physical acoustics, auditory apparatus, sound perception, development of musical skills, nature of musical feeling, host of other topics. 88 figures. 408pp. 5⅜ × 8½. 21851-1 Pa. $9.95

THE PHILOSOPHY OF HISTORY, Georg W. Hegel. Great classic of Western thought develops concept that history is not chance but rational process, the evolution of freedom. 457pp. 5⅜ × 8½.　20112-0 Pa. $9.95

THE BOOK OF TEA, Kakuzo Okakura. Minor classic of the Orient: entertaining, charming explanation, interpretation of traditional Japanese culture in terms of tea ceremony. 94pp. 5⅜ × 8½.　20070-1 Pa. $3.95

LIFE IN ANCIENT EGYPT, Adolf Erman. Fullest, most thorough, detailed older account with much not in more recent books, domestic life, religion, magic, medicine, commerce, much more. Many illustrations reproduce tomb paintings, carvings, hieroglyphs, etc. 597pp. 5⅜ × 8½.　22632-8 Pa. $10.95

SUNDIALS, Their Theory and Construction, Albert Waugh. Far and away the best, most thorough coverage of ideas, mathematics concerned, types, construction, adjusting anywhere. Simple, nontechnical treatment allows even children to build several of these dials. Over 100 illustrations. 230pp. 5⅜ × 8½.　22947-5 Pa. $7.95

DYNAMICS OF FLUIDS IN POROUS MEDIA, Jacob Bear. For advanced students of ground water hydrology, soil mechanics and physics, drainage and irrigation engineering, and more. 335 illustrations. Exercises, with answers. 784pp. 6⅛ × 9¼.　65675-6 Pa. $19.95

SONGS OF EXPERIENCE: Facsimile Reproduction with 26 Plates in Full Color, William Blake. 26 full-color plates from a rare 1826 edition. Includes "The Tyger," "London," "Holy Thursday," and other poems. Printed text of poems. 48pp. 5¼ × 7.
24636-1 Pa. $4.95

OLD-TIME VIGNETTES IN FULL COLOR, Carol Belanger Grafton (ed.). Over 390 charming, often sentimental illustrations, selected from archives of Victorian graphics—pretty women posing, children playing, food, flowers, kittens and puppies, smiling cherubs, birds and butterflies, much more. All copyright-free. 48pp. 9¼ × 12¼.　27269-9 Pa. $5.95

PERSPECTIVE FOR ARTISTS, Rex Vicat Cole. Depth, perspective of sky and sea, shadows, much more, not usually covered. 391 diagrams, 81 reproductions of drawings and paintings. 279pp. 5⅜ × 8½. 22487-2 Pa. $6.95

DRAWING THE LIVING FIGURE, Joseph Sheppard. Innovative approach to artistic anatomy focuses on specifics of surface anatomy, rather than muscles and bones. Over 170 drawings of live models in front, back and side views, and in widely varying poses. Accompanying diagrams. 177 illustrations. Introduction. Index. 144pp. 8⅜ × 11¼. 26723-7 Pa. $8.95

GOTHIC AND OLD ENGLISH ALPHABETS: 100 Complete Fonts, Dan X. Solo. Add power, elegance to posters, signs, other graphics with 100 stunning copyright-free alphabets: Blackstone, Dolbey, Germania, 97 more—including many lower-case, numerals, punctuation marks. 104pp. 8⅛ × 11. 24695-7 Pa. $8.95

HOW TO DO BEADWORK, Mary White. Fundamental book on craft from simple projects to five-bead chains and woven works. 106 illustrations. 142pp. 5⅜ × 8. 20697-1 Pa. $4.95

THE BOOK OF WOOD CARVING, Charles Marshall Sayers. Finest book for beginners discusses fundamentals and offers 34 designs. "Absolutely first rate . . . well thought out and well executed."—E. J. Tangerman. 118pp. 7¾ × 10⅝. 23654-4 Pa. $5.95

ILLUSTRATED CATALOG OF CIVIL WAR MILITARY GOODS: Union Army Weapons, Insignia, Uniform Accessories, and Other Equipment, Schuyler, Hartley, and Graham. Rare, profusely illustrated 1846 catalog includes Union Army uniform and dress regulations, arms and ammunition, coats, insignia, flags, swords, rifles, etc. 226 illustrations. 160pp. 9 × 12. 24939-5 Pa. $10.95

WOMEN'S FASHIONS OF THE EARLY 1900s: An Unabridged Republication of "New York Fashions, 1909," National Cloak & Suit Co. Rare catalog of mail-order fashions documents women's and children's clothing styles shortly after the turn of the century. Captions offer full descriptions, prices. Invaluable resource for fashion, costume historians. Approximately 725 illustrations. 128pp. 8⅜ × 11¼. 27276-1 Pa. $11.95

THE 1912 AND 1915 GUSTAV STICKLEY FURNITURE CATALOGS, Gustav Stickley. With over 200 detailed illustrations and descriptions, these two catalogs are essential reading and reference materials and identification guides for Stickley furniture. Captions cite materials, dimensions and prices. 112pp. 6½ × 9¼. 26676-1 Pa. $9.95

EARLY AMERICAN LOCOMOTIVES, John H. White, Jr. Finest locomotive engravings from early 19th century: historical (1804–74), main-line (after 1870), special, foreign, etc. 147 plates. 142pp. 11⅜ × 8¼. 22772-3 Pa. $10.95

THE TALL SHIPS OF TODAY IN PHOTOGRAPHS, Frank O. Braynard. Lavishly illustrated tribute to nearly 100 majestic contemporary sailing vessels: Amerigo Vespucci, Clearwater, Constitution, Eagle, Mayflower, Sea Cloud, Victory, many more. Authoritative captions provide statistics, background on each ship. 190 black-and-white photographs and illustrations. Introduction. 128pp. 8⅞ × 11¾. 27163-3 Pa. $13.95

EARLY NINETEENTH-CENTURY CRAFTS AND TRADES, Peter Stockham (ed.). Extremely rare 1807 volume describes to youngsters the crafts and trades of the day: brickmaker, weaver, dressmaker, bookbinder, ropemaker, saddler, many more. Quaint prose, charming illustrations for each craft. 20 black-and-white line illustrations. 192pp. 4⅝ × 6. 27293-1 Pa. $4.95

VICTORIAN FASHIONS AND COSTUMES FROM HARPER'S BAZAR, 1867–1898, Stella Blum (ed.). Day costumes, evening wear, sports clothes, shoes, hats, other accessories in over 1,000 detailed engravings. 320pp. 9⅜ × 12¼. 22990-4 Pa. $13.95

GUSTAV STICKLEY, THE CRAFTSMAN, Mary Ann Smith. Superb study surveys broad scope of Stickley's achievement, especially in architecture. Design philosophy, rise and fall of the Craftsman empire, descriptions and floor plans for many Craftsman houses, more. 86 black-and-white halftones. 31 line illustrations. Introduction. 208pp. 6½ × 9¼. 27210-9 Pa. $9.95

THE LONG ISLAND RAIL ROAD IN EARLY PHOTOGRAPHS, Ron Ziel. Over 220 rare photos, informative text document origin (1844) and development of rail service on Long Island. Vintage views of early trains, locomotives, stations, passengers, crews, much more. Captions. 8⅞ × 11¾. 26301-0 Pa. $13.95

THE BOOK OF OLD SHIPS: From Egyptian Galleys to Clipper Ships, Henry B. Culver. Superb, authoritative history of sailing vessels, with 80 magnificent line illustrations. Galley, bark, caravel, longship, whaler, many more. Detailed, informative text on each vessel by noted naval historian. Introduction. 256pp. 5⅜ × 8½. 27332-6 Pa. $6.95

TEN BOOKS ON ARCHITECTURE, Vitruvius. The most important book ever written on architecture. Early Roman aesthetics, technology, classical orders, site selection, all other aspects. Morgan translation. 331pp. 5⅜ × 8½. 20645-9 Pa. $8.95

THE HUMAN FIGURE IN MOTION, Eadweard Muybridge. More than 4,500 stopped-action photos, in action series, showing undraped men, women, children jumping, lying down, throwing, sitting, wrestling, carrying, etc. 390pp. 7⅞ × 10⅝. 20204-6 Clothbd. $24.95

TREES OF THE EASTERN AND CENTRAL UNITED STATES AND CANADA, William M. Harlow. Best one-volume guide to 140 trees. Full descriptions, woodlore, range, etc. Over 600 illustrations. Handy size. 288pp. 4½ × 6⅜. 20395-6 Pa. $5.95

SONGS OF WESTERN BIRDS, Dr. Donald J. Borror. Complete song and call repertoire of 60 western species, including flycatchers, juncoes, cactus wrens, many more—includes fully illustrated booklet. Cassette and manual 99913-0 $8.95

GROWING AND USING HERBS AND SPICES, Milo Miloradovich. Versatile handbook provides all the information needed for cultivation and use of all the herbs and spices available in North America. 4 illustrations. Index. Glossary. 236pp. 5⅜ × 8½. 25058-X Pa. $6.95

BIG BOOK OF MAZES AND LABYRINTHS, Walter Shepherd. 50 mazes and labyrinths in all—classical, solid, ripple, and more—in one great volume. Perfect inexpensive puzzler for clever youngsters. Full solutions. 112pp. 8⅛ × 11. 22951-3 Pa. $4.95

PIANO TUNING, J. Cree Fischer. Clearest, best book for beginner, amateur. Simple repairs, raising dropped notes, tuning by easy method of flattened fifths. No previous skills needed. 4 illustrations. 201pp. 5⅜ × 8½.　　23267-0 Pa. $5.95

A SOURCE BOOK IN THEATRICAL HISTORY, A. M. Nagler. Contemporary observers on acting, directing, make-up, costuming, stage props, machinery, scene design, from Ancient Greece to Chekhov. 611pp. 5⅜ × 8½.　　20515-0 Pa. $11.95

THE COMPLETE NONSENSE OF EDWARD LEAR, Edward Lear. All nonsense limericks, zany alphabets, Owl and Pussycat, songs, nonsense botany, etc., illustrated by Lear. Total of 320pp. 5⅜ × 8½. (USO)　　20167-8 Pa. $6.95

VICTORIAN PARLOUR POETRY: An Annotated Anthology, Michael R. Turner. 117 gems by Longfellow, Tennyson, Browning, many lesser-known poets. "The Village Blacksmith," "Curfew Must Not Ring Tonight," "Only a Baby Small," dozens more, often difficult to find elsewhere. Index of poets, titles, first lines. xxiii + 325pp. 5⅜ × 8¼.　　27044-0 Pa. $8.95

DUBLINERS, James Joyce. Fifteen stories offer vivid, tightly focused observations of the lives of Dublin's poorer classes. At least one, "The Dead," is considered a masterpiece. Reprinted complete and unabridged from standard edition. 160pp. 5³⁄₁₆ × 8¼.　　26870-5 Pa. $1.00

THE HAUNTED MONASTERY and THE CHINESE MAZE MURDERS, Robert van Gulik. Two full novels by van Gulik, set in 7th-century China, continue adventures of Judge Dee and his companions. An evil Taoist monastery, seemingly supernatural events; overgrown topiary maze hides strange crimes. 27 illustrations. 328pp. 5⅜ × 8½.　　23502-5 Pa. $7.95

THE BOOK OF THE SACRED MAGIC OF ABRAMELIN THE MAGE, translated by S. MacGregor Mathers. Medieval manuscript of ceremonial magic. Basic document in Aleister Crowley, Golden Dawn groups. 268pp. 5⅜ × 8½.
23211-5 Pa. $8.95

NEW RUSSIAN-ENGLISH AND ENGLISH-RUSSIAN DICTIONARY, M. A. O'Brien. This is a remarkably handy Russian dictionary, containing a surprising amount of information, including over 70,000 entries. 366pp. 4½ × 6⅛.
20208-9 Pa. $9.95

HISTORIC HOMES OF THE AMERICAN PRESIDENTS, Second, Revised Edition, Irvin Haas. A traveler's guide to American Presidential homes, most open to the public, depicting and describing homes occupied by every American President from George Washington to George Bush. With visiting hours, admission charges, travel routes. 175 photographs. Index. 160pp. 8¼ × 11. 26751-2 Pa. $10.95

NEW YORK IN THE FORTIES, Andreas Feininger. 162 brilliant photographs by the well-known photographer, formerly with *Life* magazine. Commuters, shoppers, Times Square at night, much else from city at its peak. Captions by John von Hartz. 181pp. 9¼ × 10¾.　　23585-8 Pa. $12.95

INDIAN SIGN LANGUAGE, William Tomkins. Over 525 signs developed by Sioux and other tribes. Written instructions and diagrams. Also 290 pictographs. 111pp. 6⅛ × 9¼.　　22029-X Pa. $3.50

ANATOMY: A Complete Guide for Artists, Joseph Sheppard. A master of figure drawing shows artists how to render human anatomy convincingly. Over 460 illustrations. 224pp. 8⅜ × 11¼. 27279-6 Pa. $10.95

MEDIEVAL CALLIGRAPHY: Its History and Technique, Marc Drogin. Spirited history, comprehensive instruction manual covers 13 styles (ca. 4th century thru 15th). Excellent photographs; directions for duplicating medieval techniques with modern tools. 224pp. 8⅜ × 11¼. 26142-5 Pa. $11.95

DRIED FLOWERS: How to Prepare Them, Sarah Whitlock and Martha Rankin. Complete instructions on how to use silica gel, meal and borax, perlite aggregate, sand and borax, glycerine and water to create attractive permanent flower arrangements. 12 illustrations. 32pp. 5⅜ × 8½. 21802-3 Pa. $1.00

EASY-TO-MAKE BIRD FEEDERS FOR WOODWORKERS, Scott D. Campbell. Detailed, simple-to-use guide for designing, constructing, caring for and using feeders. Text, illustrations for 12 classic and contemporary designs. 96pp. 5⅜ × 8½. 25847-5 Pa. $2.95

OLD-TIME CRAFTS AND TRADES, Peter Stockham. An 1807 book created to teach children about crafts and trades open to them as future careers. It describes in detailed, nontechnical terms 24 different occupations, among them coachmaker, gardener, hairdresser, lacemaker, shoemaker, wheelwright, copper-plate printer, milliner, trunkmaker, merchant and brewer. Finely detailed engravings illustrate each occupation. 192pp. 4⅝ × 6. 27398-9 Pa. $4.95

THE HISTORY OF UNDERCLOTHES, C. Willett Cunnington and Phyllis Cunnington. Fascinating, well-documented survey covering six centuries of English undergarments, enhanced with over 100 illustrations: 12th-century laced-up bodice, footed long drawers (1795), 19th-century bustles, 19th-century corsets for men, Victorian "bust improvers," much more. 272pp. 5⅝ × 8¼. 27124-2 Pa. $9.95

ARTS AND CRAFTS FURNITURE: The Complete Brooks Catalog of 1912, Brooks Manufacturing Co. Photos and detailed descriptions of more than 150 now very collectible furniture designs from the Arts and Crafts movement depict davenports, settees, buffets, desks, tables, chairs, bedsteads, dressers and more, all built of solid, quarter-sawed oak. Invaluable for students and enthusiasts of antiques, Americana and the decorative arts. 80pp. 6½ × 9¼. 27471-3 Pa. $7.95

HOW WE INVENTED THE AIRPLANE: An Illustrated History, Orville Wright. Fascinating firsthand account covers early experiments, construction of planes and motors, first flights, much more. Introduction and commentary by Fred C. Kelly. 76 photographs. 96pp. 8¼ × 11. 25662-6 Pa. $8.95

THE ARTS OF THE SAILOR: Knotting, Splicing and Ropework, Hervey Garrett Smith. Indispensable shipboard reference covers tools, basic knots and useful hitches; handsewing and canvas work, more. Over 100 illustrations. Delightful reading for sea lovers. 256pp. 5⅜ × 8½. 26440-8 Pa. $7.95

FRANK LLOYD WRIGHT'S FALLINGWATER: The House and Its History, Second, Revised Edition, Donald Hoffmann. A total revision—both in text and illustrations—of the standard document on Fallingwater, the boldest, most personal architectural statement of Wright's mature years, updated with valuable new material from the recently opened Frank Lloyd Wright Archives. "Fascinating"—*The New York Times*. 116 illustrations. 128pp. 9¼ × 10¾. 27430-6 Pa. $10.95

PHOTOGRAPHIC SKETCHBOOK OF THE CIVIL WAR, Alexander Gardner. 100 photos taken on field during the Civil War. Famous shots of Manassas, Harper's Ferry, Lincoln, Richmond, slave pens, etc. 244pp. 10⅝ × 8¼.
22731-6 Pa. $9.95

FIVE ACRES AND INDEPENDENCE, Maurice G. Kains. Great back-to-the-land classic explains basics of self-sufficient farming. The one book to get. 95 illustrations. 397pp. 5⅜ × 8½. 20974-1 Pa. $7.95

SONGS OF EASTERN BIRDS, Dr. Donald J. Borror. Songs and calls of 60 species most common to eastern U.S.: warblers, woodpeckers, flycatchers, thrushes, larks, many more in high-quality recording. Cassette and manual 99912-2 $8.95

A MODERN HERBAL, Margaret Grieve. Much the fullest, most exact, most useful compilation of herbal material. Gigantic alphabetical encyclopedia, from aconite to zedoary, gives botanical information, medical properties, folklore, economic uses, much else. Indispensable to serious reader. 161 illustrations. 888pp. 6½ × 9¼. 2-vol. set. (USO) Vol. I: 22798-7 Pa. $9.95
Vol. II: 22799-5 Pa. $9.95

HIDDEN TREASURE MAZE BOOK, Dave Phillips. Solve 34 challenging mazes accompanied by heroic tales of adventure. Evil dragons, people-eating plants, bloodthirsty giants, many more dangerous adversaries lurk at every twist and turn. 34 mazes, stories, solutions. 48pp. 8¼ × 11. 24566-7 Pa. $2.95

LETTERS OF W. A. MOZART, Wolfgang A. Mozart. Remarkable letters show bawdy wit, humor, imagination, musical insights, contemporary musical world; includes some letters from Leopold Mozart. 276pp. 5⅜ × 8½. 22859-2 Pa. $7.95

BASIC PRINCIPLES OF CLASSICAL BALLET, Agrippina Vaganova. Great Russian theoretician, teacher explains methods for teaching classical ballet. 118 illustrations. 175pp. 5⅜ × 8½. 22036-2 Pa. $4.95

THE JUMPING FROG, Mark Twain. Revenge edition. The original story of The Celebrated Jumping Frog of Calaveras County, a hapless French translation, and Twain's hilarious "retranslation" from the French. 12 illustrations. 66pp. 5⅜ × 8½. 22686-7 Pa. $3.95

BEST REMEMBERED POEMS, Martin Gardner (ed.). The 126 poems in this superb collection of 19th- and 20th-century British and American verse range from Shelley's "To a Skylark" to the impassioned "Renascence" of Edna St. Vincent Millay and to Edward Lear's whimsical "The Owl and the Pussycat." 224pp. 5⅜ × 8½. 27165-X Pa. $4.95

COMPLETE SONNETS, William Shakespeare. Over 150 exquisite poems deal with love, friendship, the tyranny of time, beauty's evanescence, death and other themes in language of remarkable power, precision and beauty. Glossary of archaic terms. 80pp. 5³⁄₁₆ × 8¼. 26686-9 Pa. $1.00

BODIES IN A BOOKSHOP, R. T. Campbell. Challenging mystery of blackmail and murder with ingenious plot and superbly drawn characters. In the best tradition of British suspense fiction. 192pp. 5⅜ × 8½. 24720-1 Pa. $5.95

THE WIT AND HUMOR OF OSCAR WILDE, Alvin Redman (ed.). More than 1,000 ripostes, paradoxes, wisecracks: Work is the curse of the drinking classes; I can resist everything except temptation; etc. 258pp. 5⅜ × 8½. 20602-5 Pa. $5.95

SHAKESPEARE LEXICON AND QUOTATION DICTIONARY, Alexander Schmidt. Full definitions, locations, shades of meaning in every word in plays and poems. More than 50,000 exact quotations. 1,485pp. 6½ × 9¼. 2-vol. set.
Vol. I: 22726-X Pa. $16.95
Vol. 2: 22727-8 Pa. $15.95

SELECTED POEMS, Emily Dickinson. Over 100 best-known, best-loved poems by one of America's foremost poets, reprinted from authoritative early editions. No comparable edition at this price. Index of first lines. 64pp. 5³⁄₁₆ × 8¼.
26466-1 Pa. $1.00

CELEBRATED CASES OF JUDGE DEE (DEE GOONG AN), translated by Robert van Gulik. Authentic 18th-century Chinese detective novel; Dee and associates solve three interlocked cases. Led to van Gulik's own stories with same characters. Extensive introduction. 9 illustrations. 237pp. 5⅜ × 8½.
23337-5 Pa. $6.95

THE MALLEUS MALEFICARUM OF KRAMER AND SPRENGER, translated by Montague Summers. Full text of most important witchhunter's "bible," used by both Catholics and Protestants. 278pp. 6⅝ × 10. 22802-9 Pa. $11.95

SPANISH STORIES/CUENTOS ESPAÑOLES: A Dual-Language Book, Angel Flores (ed.). Unique format offers 13 great stories in Spanish by Cervantes, Borges, others. Faithful English translations on facing pages. 352pp. 5⅜ × 8½.
25399-6 Pa. $8.95

THE CHICAGO WORLD'S FAIR OF 1893: A Photographic Record, Stanley Appelbaum (ed.). 128 rare photos show 200 buildings, Beaux-Arts architecture, Midway, original Ferris Wheel, Edison's kinetoscope, more. Architectural emphasis; full text. 116pp. 8¼ × 11. 23990-X Pa. $9.95

OLD QUEENS, N.Y., IN EARLY PHOTOGRAPHS, Vincent F. Seyfried and William Asadorian. Over 160 rare photographs of Maspeth, Jamaica, Jackson Heights, and other areas. Vintage views of DeWitt Clinton mansion, 1939 World's Fair and more. Captions. 192pp. 8⅞ × 11. 26358-4 Pa. $12.95

CAPTURED BY THE INDIANS: 15 Firsthand Accounts, 1750–1870, Frederick Drimmer. Astounding true historical accounts of grisly torture, bloody conflicts, relentless pursuits, miraculous escapes and more, by people who lived to tell the tale. 384pp. 5⅜ × 8½. 24901-8 Pa. $8.95

THE WORLD'S GREAT SPEECHES, Lewis Copeland and Lawrence W. Lamm (eds.). Vast collection of 278 speeches of Greeks to 1970. Powerful and effective models; unique look at history. 842pp. 5⅜ × 8½. 20468-5 Pa. $14.95

THE BOOK OF THE SWORD, Sir Richard F. Burton. Great Victorian scholar/adventurer's eloquent, erudite history of the "queen of weapons"—from prehistory to early Roman Empire. Evolution and development of early swords, variations (sabre, broadsword, cutlass, scimitar, etc.), much more. 336pp. 6⅛ × 9¼. 25434-8 Pa. $8.95

AUTOBIOGRAPHY: The Story of My Experiments with Truth, Mohandas K. Gandhi. Boyhood, legal studies, purification, the growth of the Satyagraha (nonviolent protest) movement. Critical, inspiring work of the man responsible for the freedom of India. 480pp. 5⅜ × 8½. (USO) 24593-4 Pa. $8.95

CELTIC MYTHS AND LEGENDS, T. W. Rolleston. Masterful retelling of Irish and Welsh stories and tales. Cuchulain, King Arthur, Deirdre, the Grail, many more. First paperback edition. 58 full-page illustrations. 512pp. 5⅜ × 8½.
26507-2 Pa. $9.95

THE PRINCIPLES OF PSYCHOLOGY, William James. Famous long course complete, unabridged. Stream of thought, time perception, memory, experimental methods; great work decades ahead of its time. 94 figures. 1,391pp. 5⅜ × 8½. 2-vol. set.
Vol. I: 20381-6 Pa. $12.95
Vol. II: 20382-4 Pa. $12.95

THE WORLD AS WILL AND REPRESENTATION, Arthur Schopenhauer. Definitive English translation of Schopenhauer's life work, correcting more than 1,000 errors, omissions in earlier translations. Translated by E. F. J. Payne. Total of 1,269pp. 5⅜ × 8½. 2-vol. set. Vol. 1: 21761-2 Pa. $11.95
Vol. 2: 21762-0 Pa. $11.95

MAGIC AND MYSTERY IN TIBET, Madame Alexandra David-Neel. Experiences among lamas, magicians, sages, sorcerers, Bonpa wizards. A true psychic discovery. 32 illustrations. 321pp. 5⅜ × 8½. (USO) 22682-4 Pa. $8.95

THE EGYPTIAN BOOK OF THE DEAD, E. A. Wallis Budge. Complete reproduction of Ani's papyrus, finest ever found. Full hieroglyphic text, interlinear transliteration, word-for-word translation, smooth translation. 533pp. 6½ × 9¼.
21866-X Pa. $9.95

MATHEMATICS FOR THE NONMATHEMATICIAN, Morris Kline. Detailed, college-level treatment of mathematics in cultural and historical context, with numerous exercises. Recommended Reading Lists. Tables. Numerous figures. 641pp. 5⅜ × 8½. 24823-2 Pa. $11.95

THEORY OF WING SECTIONS: Including a Summary of Airfoil Data, Ira H. Abbott and A. E. von Doenhoff. Concise compilation of subsonic aerodynamic characteristics of NACA wing sections, plus description of theory. 350pp. of tables. 693pp. 5⅜ × 8½. 60586-8 Pa. $14.95

THE RIME OF THE ANCIENT MARINER, Gustave Doré, S. T. Coleridge. Doré's finest work; 34 plates capture moods, subtleties of poem. Flawless full-size reproductions printed on facing pages with authoritative text of poem. "Beautiful. Simply beautiful."—*Publisher's Weekly*. 77pp. 9¼ × 12. 22305-1 Pa. $6.95

NORTH AMERICAN INDIAN DESIGNS FOR ARTISTS AND CRAFTSPEOPLE, Eva Wilson. Over 360 authentic copyright-free designs adapted from Navajo blankets, Hopi pottery, Sioux buffalo hides, more. Geometrics, symbolic figures, plant and animal motifs, etc. 128pp. 8⅜ × 11. (EUK) 25341-4 Pa. $7.95

SCULPTURE: Principles and Practice, Louis Slobodkin. Step-by-step approach to clay, plaster, metals, stone; classical and modern. 253 drawings, photos. 255pp. 8⅛ × 11. 22960-2 Pa. $10.95

1-1   52%   2-0   48%
3-1   50%   2-2   40%   4-0   10%
4-2   48%   3-3   36%

2-1   78%   3-0   22%
3-2   68%   4-1   28%   5-0
4-3   62%   5-2   31%

CATALOG OF DOVER BOOKS

THE INFLUENCE OF SEA POWER UPON HISTORY, 1660–1783, A. T. Mahan. Influential classic of naval history and tactics still used as text in war colleges. First paperback edition. 4 maps. 24 battle plans. 640pp. 5⅜ × 8½.
25509-3 Pa. $12.95

THE STORY OF THE TITANIC AS TOLD BY ITS SURVIVORS, Jack Winocour (ed.). What it was really like. Panic, despair, shocking inefficiency, and a little heroism. More thrilling than any fictional account. 26 illustrations. 320pp. 5⅜ × 8½. 20610-6 Pa. $8.95

FAIRY AND FOLK TALES OF THE IRISH PEASANTRY, William Butler Yeats (ed.). Treasury of 64 tales from the twilight world of Celtic myth and legend: "The Soul Cages," "The Kildare Pooka," "King O'Toole and his Goose," many more. Introduction and Notes by W. B. Yeats. 352pp. 5⅜ × 8½. 26941-8 Pa. $8.95

BUDDHIST MAHAYANA TEXTS, E. B. Cowell and Others (eds.). Superb, accurate translations of basic documents in Mahayana Buddhism, highly important in history of religions. The Buddha-karita of Asvaghosha, Larger Sukhavativyuha, more. 448pp. 5⅜ × 8½. 25552-2 Pa. $9.95

ONE TWO THREE . . . INFINITY: Facts and Speculations of Science, George Gamow. Great physicist's fascinating, readable overview of contemporary science: number theory, relativity, fourth dimension, entropy, genes, atomic structure, much more. 128 illustrations. Index. 352pp. 5⅜ × 8½. 25664-2 Pa. $8.95

ENGINEERING IN HISTORY, Richard Shelton Kirby, et al. Broad, nontechnical survey of history's major technological advances: birth of Greek science, industrial revolution, electricity and applied science, 20th-century automation, much more. 181 illustrations. ". . . excellent . . ."—Isis. Bibliography. vii + 530pp. 5⅜ × 8¼.
26412-2 Pa. $14.95

Prices subject to change without notice.

Available at your book dealer or write for free catalog to Dept. GI, Dover Publications, Inc., 31 East 2nd St., Mineola, N.Y. 11501. Dover publishes more than 500 books each year on science, elementary and advanced mathematics, biology, music, art, literary history, social sciences and other areas.